Advance praise from India for *Himalaya Bound*:

"A perceptive account. Evocative and full of drama. *Himalaya Bound* is an important contribution to mountain narratives, along with being a compelling memoir of understanding between cultures. At heart, this is a story of friendship and trust, told with the kind of integrity and compassion that often seems absent in our world today."

—*Biblio: A Review of Books*

"A deeply personal account and an important testimony to a way of life—and a way of interacting with animals—that is under a lot of pressure not only in India but around the world. Don't miss this unique and immensely readable tale about people that do more for animal welfare than anybody else."   —*The Hindustan Times*

"A rare glimpse into the hidden world of a tribe of vegetarian Muslims who risk their lives for their animals."   —*The Times of India*

"Compassionate, sensitive, and keenly attuned to the challenges confronted by traditional ways of life around the world. Benanav forces us to ask important questions about the relationship between man and nature in India today."

—Akash Kapur, author of *India Becoming*

"Closely observed and sympathetically told, Benanav captures the very best of modern-day travel writing. Benanav serves as the very best of guides on this most unique of journeys."   —Oliver Balch, author of *India Rising*

"Captivating. Poignant. Inspiring. Benanav proffers an extraordinary insight into the lives of an age-old tribal culture and the multifarious challenges it faces in 21st-century India."   —Sarina Singh, *The Lonely Planet Guidebook to India*

"An enchanting read, *Himalaya Bound* is a great and important book providing insight into a vanishing way of life."   —Ilse Köhler-Rollefson, author of *Camel Karma: Twenty Years Among India's Camel Nomads*

HIMALAYA BOUND

ONE FAMILY'S QUEST TO SAVE THEIR ANIMALS—AND AN ANCIENT WAY OF LIFE

MICHAEL BENANAV

PEGASUS BOOKS
NEW YORK LONDON

For Sharafat

❧

HIMALAYA BOUND

Pegasus Books Ltd.
148 W 37th Street, 13th Floor
New York, NY 10018

Copyright © 2018 by Michael Benanav

All images © Michael Benanav

First Pegasus Books edition January 2018

Interior design by Maria Fernandez

Library of Congress Cataloging-in-Publication Data is available.

ISBN: 978-1-68177-622-4

10 9 8 7 6 5 4 3 2 1

Printed in the United States of America
Distributed by W. W. Norton & Company, Inc.
www.pegasusbooks.us

CONTENTS

FAMILY TREE

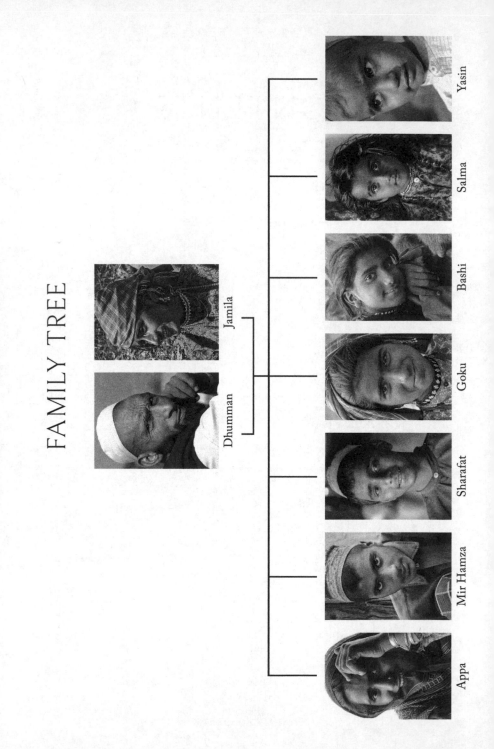

Dhumman — Jamila

Appa · Mir Hamza · Sharafat · Goku · Bashi · Salma · Yasin

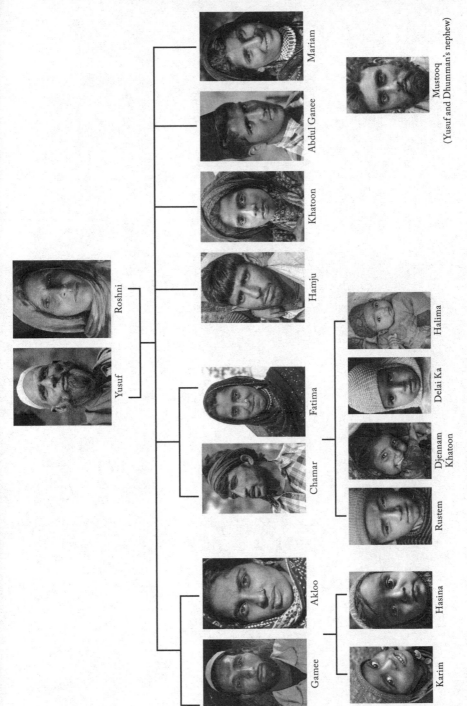

Yusuf   Roshni

Mariam   Abdul Ganee   Khatoon   Hamju

Mustooq
(Yusuf and Dhumman's nephew)

Fatima   Chamar

Rustem   Djennam
Khatoon   Delai Ka   Halima

Akloo   Gamee

Karim   Hasina

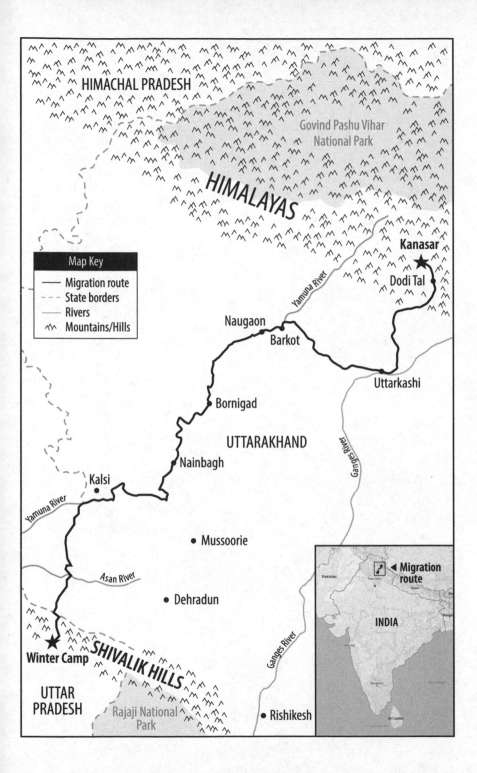

1

INTO THE FOREST

I n a one-room hut in the middle of the forest, Dhumman
knelt and prayed, facing west, towards Mecca. Performing
the ritual prostrations, his shadow rose and fell upon a
mud-plastered wall that glowed in the flickering light cast by
a crackling cook fire and a single kerosene lamp. His rhythmic
chanting filled the hut with a low, resonant hum. It was two
o'clock in the morning.

Sitting on the dirt floor next to an earthen hearth, Dhumman's
twenty-two-year-old daughter watched the morning chai simmer

while she was churning butter—pulling back and forth on a rope that was wrapped around a wooden spindle, which sloshed vigorously in a narrow-mouthed pot filled with milk. Her teenaged brothers and sister, awakened by the demands of the day much earlier than usual, moved sluggishly around the hut, as though caught in the tendrils of lingering dreams. With their feet, they gently prodded their youngest siblings, who were still asleep on the floor. It was time to pack the bedrolls. It was time to get going.

The voice of their mother, Jamila, acted like a tonic, snapping her children out of their drowsy trance. At her request, the two eldest boys, flashlights in hand, left the hut to fetch the pack animals. Meanwhile, Jamila methodically placed the last of the family's belongings into saddlebags of thickly woven horsehair, which she then tied shut. When the young men returned, they carried the bags outside and loaded them onto the two horses and three bulls that they had parked by the door. Dhumman interrupted his prayers to issue instructions to his sons, reminding them to make sure that everything was properly balanced and well secured on the animals' backs. The brothers, aged nineteen and sixteen, looked at each other and rolled their eyes; they knew perfectly well what they were doing.

In the darkness of the jungle, cowbells clanged, crickets chirped, and monkeys howled in the trees.

The mood in the hut was charged with the same kind of tension and excitement that families typically feel just before leaving on a trip. But there was nothing typical about the trip this family was about to take. Well aware of this, Dhumman closed his devotions by asking Allah to ease the difficult journey on which they were about to embark. Though he had travelled this route every spring since the year he was born, and was intimately familiar with the myriad challenges his family and their herd of buffaloes normally face on their annual migration, he had reason to fear that this year—2009—would be unusually tough.

꧁

Dhumman and his family belong to the Van Gujjar tribe and, like all Van Gujjars who are still able to practice their traditional way of life, they are nomadic water buffalo herders. They live year-round in the wilderness—never in villages—grazing their livestock on the vegetation that grows in the jungles and mountains of northern India. The tribe spends winters, from October to April, in the Shivalik Hills—a low but rugged range that arcs through parts of the states of Uttar Pradesh, Uttarakhand, and Himachal Pradesh. Amid the dense forest, each Van Gujjar family settles into a base camp; every day, from their huts of sticks and mud, they roam over gnarled sedimentary topography, through a tangle of deciduous trees and shrubs, feeding their buffaloes on the abundant foliage.

In the month of March, however, heat begins to sear the Shivaliks. By mid-April, temperatures soar to 115 degrees. The creeks that snake through the range run dry. As though baking in an oven, the forest canopy turns brown. Leaves wither, die, and fall from the trees. The once-verdant hills go bald. With little left for their buffaloes to eat or drink, the Van Gujjars must move elsewhere to survive. They pack their entire households onto horses and bulls and hike their herds up to the Himalayas, aiming for high alpine meadows that are flush with grass throughout the summer.

They stay in the mountains until autumn. Then, with temperatures plunging and snow beginning to fall, they retreat back down to the Shivaliks. By the time they reach there, usually in early October, they find the low hills bursting with life once again, the thick forest canopy regenerated over the previous months by the moisture delivered during the summer monsoon, the water sources recharged. With plenty to sustain their animals, they stay in the jungle—each family often returning to the very same hut that they occupied the previous winter—until springtime temperatures drive them back to the Himalayas. This migratory pattern—up in spring and down in autumn—has been practiced by Van Gujjars in this part of India for many, many generations.

It's believed that the first Van Gujjars came to the Shivalik region, probably from Kashmir, some 1,500 years ago. No one knows exactly when or exactly why, but some in the tribe say their people were invited by the local raja; he'd been travelling in Kashmir and was so impressed by the Van Gujjars, their buffalo herds, and the high quality of their milk, that he asked them to come live in his kingdom.

Other Van Gujjars may tell you that they themselves are of royal blood. Once upon a time, they say, a prince fell in love-at-first-sight with a beautiful Van Gujjar woman who was herding buffaloes in Punjab. He asked her to marry, so she moved to his kingdom, bringing some animals with her. But when winter turned to spring, her buffaloes couldn't tolerate the smothering heat: they fell ill, and a few died. Alarmed by their suffering, the new princess did what her family always did during summer—she led her little herd into the high mountains to escape the swelter. When the prince begged her to return, she refused, choosing her animals over her husband and his riches. The prince couldn't bear to be without her, so he gave up his throne and joined her. From then on, they lived together in the forests, where the buffaloes—and the princess were happiest.

Their descendants, the story goes, are one of the largest Van Gujjar clans.

Today, an estimated thirty thousand Van Gujjars still dwell in the wilderness, moving seasonally between the Shivaliks and the Himalayas. They still speak their native dialect, Gujari, which is a linguistic fusion of Dogri (a Kashmiri tongue) and Punjabi.

Though changes are beginning to penetrate into their secluded forest realm—with severe cultural consequences in some places—the essence of their traditional herding lifestyle has remained largely intact through the centuries.

❦

From the earliest days of my career as a freelance writer and photojournalist, I've found myself naturally drawn to covering stories about nomadic peoples. In part, this was a holdover from my childhood fascination with Lawrence of Arabia and his relationship with the Bedouin; in my youthful imagination, I pictured myself in Lawrence's place, sitting under the tents of exotic strangers, with one foot in their tribal world, one foot in the Western world, and feeling perfectly comfortable in both. Later, as I encountered nomads first-hand during my travels to the Middle East and Central Asia, I quickly developed great respect for them and their way of life, and became intrigued by how their age-old cultures survived in the twentieth and twenty-first centuries. I also sensed, in a vague kind of way, that my fellow citizens of the modern world could probably learn a thing or two from nomadic people about how to live on Planet Earth.

From the moment I'd first heard about the Van Gujjars, I'd wanted to document their spring migration into the Himalayas. It sounded like an incredible undertaking: entire families marching with herds of water buffaloes into the highest mountains on earth. And it also seemed as though the tribe was on the cusp of irreversible change; that perhaps within a generation or two, far fewer, if any, Van Gujjars would still live in the forests, the seasonal migrations would cease, and their traditional way of life would fade away forever. Already, over the previous six decades, many Van Gujjar clans had been driven out of the jungles by government policies; today perhaps 80,000 of them live settled in villages in Punjab, Haryana, and Uttar Pradesh, with little connection to their ancestral ways.

There was something else that intrigued me about the Van Gujjars, too: the most immediate threat to their forest-dwelling, migratory lifestyle seemed to be the establishment of national parks. In the name of protecting wildlife habitat, these nomads were being pressured to abandon the wild lands on which they had lived for countless generations, to settle in villages, and to give up their buffalo herds. To my American ears, this sounded counterintuitive and strangely ironic, since national parks are meant to preserve things that are fragile and endangered, but in this case they were also threatening something fragile and endangered—the Van Gujjars' unique culture. The tribe's troubles, I saw, were wrapped in modern ethical dilemmas, which raised some compelling questions about what it means to be human on this planet.

I first met Dhumman, Jamila, and their children at their camp in the Shivalik Hills, in early April of 2009. Knowing it would be insane and inappropriate to simply show up in the Shivaliks and expect that a nomadic family would invite a random stranger to tag along with them on their migration into the Himalayas— eating, sleeping, walking and talking with them, day after day, week after week—I contacted the Society for the Promotion of Himalayan Indigenous Activities (SOPHIA), a small non-profit organization based in the city of Dehradun, which works with the Van Gujjars. I explained to its director, Praveen Kaushal (known to all as Manto), that I wanted to document the spring migration, and asked if he thought it might be possible. He assured me that it was, and told me to come to Dehradun in early April. Meanwhile, he'd think about which Van Gujjar family might be best for me to travel with, and would ask them if they'd take me along. He chose Dhumman and Jamila and, since they trusted Manto, they were open to the idea.

Manto also introduced me to someone who was willing to translate for me, since I hardly spoke any Hindi. My translator, who shuns the spotlight, has requested that he remain "humbly anonymous" in this story, so I will call him Namith, a pseudonym, and only mention him from time to time.

Dhumman, Jamila and their kids had met several foreigners through Manto before, and they knew the Swedish anthropologist, Dr. Pernille Gooch, who had spent significant amounts of time with a set of Dhumman's cousins while researching her doctoral dissertation in the late 1980s and early 1990s. So, while it was highly unusual for an American to walk into their camp in the jungle, I wasn't like a pale-skinned, camera-carrying, alien emissary from another world making first contact with a lost tribe. Which was good: I've been in places like that before, where children had burst into tears at the sight of a strange creature with a backpack entering their village, where even some adults had hidden behind trees, peeking around the trunks until they were sure of who—or what—I was. True, in all of those cases, trepidation quickly evolved into warm welcomes and offers of food and shelter, but my fast acceptance by the Van Gujjars was certainly smoothed by the other outsiders who had crossed their thresholds before me.

About a week before the migration began, I went into the Shivaliks to meet Dhumman and Jamila for the first time. Aside from simply introducing myself, I wanted to make sure that they truly felt all right about my joining them, and to ask if there was anything that I needed to know in advance.

I took a bus from Dehradun to Mohand—a village in Uttar Pradesh near the border with Uttarakhand, through which the highway linking Delhi to Dehradun passes. Small shops line both sides of the road for about one hundred yards, and Van Gujjars from the surrounding forest are often seen there picking up basic supplies or selling milk. After asking around, I found a milk merchant—who was not Van Gujjar—who was going to be driving past the part of the forest in which Dhumman lived, some ten miles west of Mohand. I hopped in the back of his battered white Mahindra pickup truck and settled in among the empty metal milk containers, which rattled violently as we maneuvered along a partially paved track that ran along the base of the Shivalik Hills.

The road was like a borderline between two very different worlds. To the left, a patchwork of villages, farms, and fields covered the fertile plains between the Ganges and Yamuna Rivers. To the right rose a forested wilderness that cut a serrated profile against a hazy sky; it looked like a rugged no-man's-land, and if I hadn't known about the Van Gujjars, I would have assumed that no man—or woman or child—lived there.

One of SOPHIA's field workers, named Nazim, waited for me along the road at a place that seemed like nowhere. We hiked a couple of miles up a wide, dry streambed—called a rao—following a dusty footpath worn among countless rounded stones. There was no water, and no shade to shield us from the scorching sun. Long after I was completely drenched in sweat, we turned up a tiny tributary that carved a narrow cleft through the hills. The foliage overhead was still mostly intact; it felt liked we'd entered a tunnel. After another half-mile, though I hadn't yet spotted Dhumman's camp, I knew we were close, thanks to the ferociously barking dog that announced our arrival; fortunately, it was tied up by the time we got there. And the tea fire was already lit.

The camp, called a *dera*, was in a small clearing alongside a dribbling creek, at the bottom of a canyon framed by steep, tree-covered slopes. The family's rectangular hut was made of sticks and logs lashed together with vines and plastered with mud. Overhead, a four-sided thatched roof rose to a peaked center ridge. Atop the walls, at about shoulder height, were wide window spaces—but no glass. And there was a large doorway, but no door. This home was always open to the sounds, smells, and breezes of the forest around it. Sometimes, I was told, animals might drop in for a visit: on more than one occasion, a deer had dashed into the hut, seeking shelter from a leopard that was pursuing it.

Made completely from natural materials, the hut felt like an organic part of the jungle. There was no plumbing: the family fetched water from a spring that trickled out of the hillside, while the buffaloes drank from a trough-like pool that Dhumman had dammed in the creek bed. There was no electricity and no phone service, no motors or machines, and no road leading to their dwelling. I was overcome by that profound sense of peacefulness that permeates places with no artifical noise.

Inside the hut, I found a single room. A partial wall separated the kitchen area, where Jamila and her older daughters cooked over fire on a hearth of rock and dirt. There was no furniture at all. The family slept on home-made bedrolls stitched from rice sacks, which were thinly stuffed with grass; at night, these would be laid out side by side on the hard adobe floor, everyone snoring and coughing and dreaming together. Now, a couple of the bedrolls were spread for Dhumman, Jamila, Nazim, Namith, and me to sit on.

Dhumman was tall and lean. His face was sharply sculpted, his eyes dark and steady. A black beard hung from his jawlines and came to a point under his chin, while his moustache was precisely trimmed to a pencil-thin line. He wore a black vest over a button-down shirt, and a plaid lungi around his waist. On this day, he wore a Muslim skullcap over his close-cropped hair, but he sometimes wore a white turban that, among Van Gujjars, is only worn by *lambardars*—tribal leaders who are part of a council that mediates disputes and tries to resolve problems. *Lambardars* don't inherit their positions, but are chosen by the community based on their character. Dhumman, I would learn, had a reputation as a wise, reasonable, and honorable man.

Like typical Van Gujjar fathers, he was the undisputed head of his household. His ideas could be questioned, especially by Jamila—whose thoughtful opinions he valued—but once he made a decision, that was that. He captained his family firmly but gently; everyone understood his expectations and followed his rules, at least while he was present. When he wasn't around, things loosened up: a relaxed mood settled over the children, and even over Jamila, who was more naturally easygoing than her husband.

Like all Van Gujjar women, Jamila wore a salwar kameez, a nose ring, a few bangles around each wrist and—often but far from always—a colorful, loose-fitting headscarf, beneath which her long hair was tied in a single braid. Her face had an ageless quality to it; with few wrinkles or creases, she seemed like she could have just as easily been in her early thirties or her late forties. Her hands, however, were rough and calloused, looking capable and reliable. While her eyes gleamed with intelligence, I quickly came to see that her smile was the true window to her soul. She was quick to laugh, even during the stressful circumstances we would soon encounter.

We drank sweet, milky chai and talked. Dhumman and Jamila seemed perfectly happy to have me join them. Dhumman's only concern was whether or not I'd be able to handle the hard living on the road. I told him about some of my previous projects, including one that took me a thousand miles through the Sahara Desert on a camel, and his doubts were quelled. He said he thought they would leave the Shivaliks after another week, so he suggested that I stay for the night, then return to Dehradun, then come back again for the migration. He promised to let me know a day or two before their departure, either by sending a message through someone else or walking out to a place where his mobile phone would have a connection.

The plan sounded perfect, and I was relieved. I'd flown to India based entirely on faith that someone I'd never met— Manto—would be able to introduce me to forest-dwelling tribal nomads who would welcome me along on their spring migration. There had been no guarantees, and I was half-prepared to arrive in the jungle and for the Van Gujjars to have no idea who I was or what I was doing there, or for them, on second thought, to decide that it would be too much trouble to put up with a foreigner and his translator on the long journey to the Himalayas. Beyond my relief that everything seemed to be falling into place, I sensed from this first meeting that I was in very good hands, though it would take some time before I could truly appreciate how fortunate I was that Manto had suggested I travel with this particular family.

I spent the rest of the day getting a taste of Van Gujjar life, taking my first steps into a world that thoroughly revolves around water buffaloes. In ways big and small, virtually everything about this nomadic culture is shaped by what's best for the animals. It's why the tribe lives in the wilderness, it's why they migrate, it's the single factor that rules the bulk of their time and energy on any given day. And for good reason: with buffalo milk as their staple food and main—often only—source of income, the well-being of every family is completely dependent on the well-being of its herd.

Dhumman explained that his family owned forty buffaloes. Each morning, they milk the ones that are lactating—perhaps ten or so at any given time. They keep a few liters for drinking, brewing tea, and making butter or yogurt, then sell the rest to an outsider who pedals a bicycle along the dirt paths that run through the Shivaliks, going from one Van Gujjar camp to the next. The doodhwallah, as he is called, fills up large metal canisters that are rigged to a rack on his bike, then rides out of the forest to bring the fresh organic milk, prized for its high fat content, to his customers in nearby villages. He doesn't pay Dhumman daily; at the beginning of each month, he hands Dhumman a cash advance. Over the next four weeks, he records how much milk he collects, then pays the balance owed.

In keeping with the core customs of his tribe, Dhumman would never dream of eating his buffaloes or selling them for slaughter. They are used exclusively as milk animals. Even male calves, which are obviously useless for dairy production, are spared the knife, and sold to farmers in nearby villages as beasts of burden for pulling carts and ploughs.

While, as Muslims, Van Gujjars have no religious taboos against consuming meat, they're traditionally vegetarian. Some scholars suggest that this may be a cultural remnant from the days before the Mughal period, when the Van Gujjars probably converted from Hinduism to Islam. But Van Gujjars say that their aversion to meat is rooted in their sense of connection to animals as fellow living beings. Likewise, though they live in the forest, they don't normally hunt. Though they share their range in the Shivaliks with tigers, leopards and elephants—often living around, or even within, wildlife sanctuaries such as Rajaji and Corbett National Parks—it's exceptionally rare for the nomads to kill a wild animal out of fear for their own safety—or for any other reason.

Their feelings for their buffaloes, however, go far beyond the cordial regard they have for other, anonymous creatures. Like the princess of legend, Van Gujjars have deep emotional attachments to their livestock. They relate to them as family members, naming each one and caring for them with genuine devotion. If a buffalo becomes ill or injured, its owners fret with concern; once, when one of the favorites in Dhumman's herd was sick, the family was so upset they could hardly eat. When a buffalo dies, the loss felt is more personal than financial; the buffalo is buried and mourned almost as though it is human. Dhumman and Jamila's son, Sharafat, told me he didn't understand why anyone would have a dog for a pet, since "buffaloes are smarter, more loyal, and more affectionate!" In fact, his family's dog was never even given a name, but just called *kutta*, since at any time it might get killed by a wild animal and the family didn't want to get too emotionally attached to it. The more I saw over time, the more it seemed to me that Van Gujjars were like doting servants to their buffalo masters.

This was especially true when it came to feeding the herd. To say that the buffaloes graze in the jungle conjures an image that's not quite accurate, since they don't browse around in the wilderness the way that cattle graze in fields. The Van Gujjars carefully control what their animals eat, knowing that the amount of milk they'll produce—along with its flavor—is determined by the type of leaves they consume. The best varieties grow on trees, rather than low-lying bushes or shrubs, but without the anatomy of giraffes, the buffaloes can't reach them. It's up to the Van Gujjars to bring the leaves down to their level.

On my first afternoon in the Shivaliks, I followed a crew of young people when they went to gather leaves, including Dhumman's twenty-two-year-old daughter, Appa; his sixteen-year-old son, Sharafat; and his seventeen-year-old niece, Mariam. They set out up the creek, each carrying a wooden-handled tool with a curved steel blade—called a *patal*—that was like a cross between a hatchet and a sickle. Their mood was light and playful and they moved quickly along the trail, talking and laughing.

When we reached the spot they had in mind, Appa, Sharafat, and Mariam scurried barefooted up the trunks of robust sal trees. They clambered far out onto the limbs, then lopped off leaf-laden boughs, which fell to the forest floor. At one point, Mariam was nearly fifty feet above the ground, poised on a narrow branch, swinging her sharp blade—and holding onto nothing other than her tool; her other hand was held out into thin air, for balance. She had the dexterity of a professional acrobat but, dressed in a gold-colored kameez with her black headscarf fluttering behind her in the wind and an expression of confidence on her face, she looked like a warrior princess; she might have been the inspiration for the flying kung-fu scenes in the movie Crouching Tiger, Hidden Dragon. I stood below and off to the side, watching in amazement as clumps of leaves plunged to the earth.

With strength and agility, they worked fast, deftly popping holes in the jungle canopy. But they never stripped any of the trees bare. They were careful to take what they could without doing any permanent damage. The last thing they wanted to do was kill the trees—they needed them to live, so they would provide ample buffalo fodder the following winter, and the winter after that, and the winter after that . . .

Aside from my awe at the physical abilities of these young Van Gujjars, I was struck by how easy-going our rapport was. There seemed to be something we had in common that was more profound, more essential, than any of our many cultural differences. Put simply, we clicked, and became fast friends. Over the course of the next two months, Appa, Sharafat, and Mariam would be among those in the family to whom I grew closest. The young women felt no need to mute their vibrant personalities behind a reserved or repressed façade, and Sharafat, who shared his thoughts openly and questioned me incisively, would become like an older/younger brother—younger, since he was, by quite a lot, and older, since I was like a child in his world.

Sharafat looked more like a boy than a man, with no signs of a moustache or beard; he had a softness to his face and a slimness to his fingers that, if his elders were any indication, would one day disappear with his youth. Mariam, depending on her mood, might look younger or older than her years, as though she could leap between childhood and adulthood, between silliness and maturity, with a turn of her head—either way, she beamed with natural beauty and cheery charisma. Appa was a self-possessed young woman with ebony irises set in almond-shaped eyes and a beauty animated by her personality—her kindness, her sense of humor, her irrepressibly independent mind.

Appa and Sharafat's fourteen-year-old sister, Goku, joined us during the tree pruning. She was a bit more cautious of the stranger in their midst, and it would take a couple of weeks before she'd fully reveal her hilariously irreverent self to me. She had come along on the leaf-lopping mission like an apprentice, trimming some of the smaller trees as she gradually built her confidence for this risky job.

Despite their well-honed skills, Van Gujjars sometimes fall from substantial heights. Every year, bones break and people die. Even Sharafat, who had mastered the arts of climbing and cutting, said that tumbling from a tree was one of his two greatest fears—you could never be completely sure that a branch wouldn't

snap beneath you, or you might simply make a mistake, mis-
judging a foothold or the way a limb might react when a bough
is lopped from it. With no safety gear of any kind, even a small
slip could be fatal.

Sharafat's other main fear: elephants, which roamed the
Shivaliks and were known for unpredictable outbursts of aggres-
siveness. They sometimes came crashing through Van Gujjar
camps, smashing huts, even trampling people. The Van Gujjars'
dogs, which are kept to protect the herd and the camp from
intruders, only make things worse: with an initial surge of
bravery, they rush out to defend their *dera*, but once they see the
size and the strength, and sometimes the tusks, of what they're
up against, they become terror-stricken, turn tail, and run, usually straight into their owner's hut, with an angry elephant in
hot pursuit. The fact that the elephant won't fit through the door
doesn't deter it from chasing the dog inside—and reducing the
hut to a pile of rubble.

Concerned that he may have frightened me, Sharafat urged
me not to worry; elephants had been in the area a couple of
months earlier, he said, but hadn't been around much lately. I
was a bit relieved, but also disappointed—despite the dangers
they posed, I wanted to see one.

When a substantial heap of branches lay on the ground,
the young Van Gujjars rapidly sliced the leaves from them and
divided them into four piles, each nearly as tall as me. The piles
were bound with vines, so they could be carried back to the *dera*.
Had this been fodder for the adult buffalos, the animals would
have been led to the leaves. But these were for the calves, which

were kept in a pen near the *dera* most of the time, partly for their safety, and partly to separate them from their mothers, so they didn't drink up all the milk.

Wanting to be helpful, I offered to carry one of the bundles of leaves. My new friends laughed, but when I convinced them that I was serious, Sharafat helped me hoist a heap onto my back, making sure that one of the vines that kept it intact was balanced on top of my head. Once I lifted it off the ground, I moved gingerly along the trail to the *dera*. Our loads were so large that, from behind, we looked like huge bushes that had pulled up their roots and started walking around. My pile was so heavy that I wondered if losing my balance might cause me to snap my neck in half.

When we reached the hut, Mariam waved goodbye, flashed a smile, and continued down the trail with her leaves, heading for her parents' *dera*, which was about a mile away, along the large, dry *rao* that I'd first hiked up with Nazim before turning into the side canyon towards Dhumman's *dera*. The rest of us dropped our burdens. We were met by Bashi, Appa and Sharafat's eleven-year-old sister, who was shy and sweet and sometimes spoke with a slight stutter. Among her many jobs, she often tended to the calves, and now she helped her brother and sisters spread the leaves for them. She wasn't yet ready to climb trees.

A bronze haze settled over the hills in late afternoon. I watched the adorable buffalo calves munch on their dinner. I watched the adult buffaloes saunter towards a line of fodder that had been cut for them at the edge of the clearing that surrounded the hut. Their charcoal-colored skin was stretched tight over corrugated ribs, angular hips, and round bellies. Meanwhile, Jamila was washing and brushing out the unruly locks of hair atop the head of her five-year-old daughter, Salma. Mir Hamza, the eldest son, was sharpening the *patals*, scraping the blades across a wet stone. Dhumman was coming up the trail from his brother's camp, using his bamboo herding *lathi* like a walking stick.

With no machines and no engines within earshot, there was little noise around the *dera*—just the wind rustling leaves, the calls of forest creatures, the occasional groan of a buffalo, and the conversations, laughter, and rare squabbles of this Van Gujjar family. As a crow flies, we were perhaps twenty miles southwest of Dehradun, where the metro area has a population of 1.3 million. But the busy city seemed light years away.

The Van Gujjars' world was so complete unto itself, with so few intrusions from outside, that I found myself slipping into a dizzy reverie. The modern world of cars and computers and shopping malls felt like some imaginary place I'd once read about in a science fiction novel, or like the hazy memory of a dream I'd had a few nights earlier. What was real was the forest.

In many ways, it was truly idyllic. But I didn't mistake the Shivaliks for Eden. Life in paradise would never be so much work! And, despite the innate peacefulness of this family's forest world, a current of anxiety was pulsing beneath its surface.

As the day was ending but before night had begun, the hut was illuminated by a lingering twilight that drifted in through the doorway and the windows. While Jamila and Appa prepared a dinner of chapati and curry, Dhumman told me about the troubling situation that he feared might end in catastrophe for his family and others. Government authorities, he said, had pledged to block some Van Gujjars from migrating, including those heading for the area where his ancestral alpine pasture was located. He'd spent every single summer of his life there, and if he was banned from it, he didn't know how he was going to feed his buffaloes.

Though I had heard about the dilemma that Dhumman was facing, the more he spoke, the more I realized how little about it I truly understood. Of course, the implications of a herd without a meadow were obvious. But I'd been unaware of just how profoundly the Van Gujjars' existence is influenced by forces other than the natural cycles of the seasons, until Dhumman began to explain.

Van Gujjars don't own any of the lands on which they live and graze; it's all common property, managed by the forest department of whatever state they happen to fall within— generally Uttarakhand, Uttar Pradesh or Himachal Pradesh. Though the tribe had been using these areas for centuries, the British Raj introduced a permitting system to administer and control nomadic movements, which was just one part of a vast colonial plan to maximize profits from forest industries across the subcontinent. Each Van Gujjar family was issued a document certifying—and cementing—where their grazing range was located and how many buffaloes they owned, which became the number they were officially authorized to keep.

To this day, the permit system remains in place. Every year, Van Gujjars have to show their papers, pay grazing taxes on their

Himalayan meadows and pay lopping taxes for their Shivalik forest use, in exchange for permission to access their traditional lands. The fees they pay are based on the amount of livestock they supposedly own, as written on their permit.

Problematically, the number of buffaloes assigned to each family's permit has been fixed since they were first allocated by the British, generations ago. Even as herds grew over time and even after India became independent—no updates have been granted. Permits may be split: a man with a permit for, say, thirty buffaloes, who has three sons, could divide his permit among them, but they would only be allowed to own ten buffaloes each. And if each of those sons had two sons, they could split their permits in half again, and so on . . . but the total number of animals on their combined permits cannot exceed the amount originally recorded by the colonial administrators.

As a result, as generations have passed and permits were split and split again, most families came to have—and need to have—more livestock than they're allowed. Even so, they were typically never blocked from using their lands. The annual permission procedure of paying a tax and getting a receipt was only a formality; the gates to the forests just required a little grease.

Black money has long been the lifeblood of the permit system. Van Gujjars expect to pay bribes when a forest ranger discovers that they have more buffaloes than they're officially allowed . . . or if something about their paperwork is amiss . . . or for any random reason that the ranger happens to invent. Because the laws are set up in such a way that the nomads inevitably break them—and because they can easily be framed for violations they didn't commit—they are vulnerable to the whims of those in power, including low-ranking, poorly-paid forest rangers, who can surely use a few extra rupees. Despite feeling regularly abused, there is a certain kind of logic to crooked systems, and for many decades the Van Gujjars took some small measure of confidence in its predictability. They had to pay a price, but they could keep living more or less as they always had.

That changed suddenly in the fall of 1992. With no warning, thousands of buffalo herders who were moving down from the Himalayas were blocked from entering a broad swath of the Shivalik Hills that stretched some forty miles southeast from the edge of Dehradun, across the River Ganga, nearly to the town of Kotdwara. This was the northern boundary line of Rajaji National Park, which had been created in 1983. Encompassing over three hundred square miles of rugged jungle terrain, Rajaji protects prime habitat for wild elephants, leopards, several species of deer, sloth bears, and a handful of tigers. But it's also the traditional home of many Van Gujjars, whose winter grazing lands were included within the park.

According to Indian law at that time, people were forbidden from living in national parks or using park resources for subsistence or profit. Though no one had challenged the Van Gujjars' rights to their winter territory in the nine years since the establishment of Rajaji, the Uttar Pradesh forest department finally decided to move against them in 1992. Rangers and policemen stopped migrating families before they reached the forests and threatened them with arrest and the confiscation of their herds if they crossed into the national park.

In a desperate effort to save themselves, the Van Gujjars protested, drawing a swirl of media attention. Legal action followed, and the Van Gujjars were temporarily allowed back into the Shivaliks. But over the next fifteen years, most of the Rajaji Park families—1,390 of them—were evicted, forced to settle in government-built villages and abandon their age-old way of life.

Dhumman's winter grazing area is west of the Rajaji zone, so his home in the Shivaliks was spared. But his summer meadow had been absorbed into Govind National Park, which is generally spoken of in conjunction with the adjacent Govind Wildlife Sanctuary, as though they are a single protected area. Together, they cover about 370 square miles surrounding the Upper Tons Valley, in the northernmost nook of Uttarakhand. Elevations range from 4265 to 20,745 feet above sea level, spanning deeply carved river canyons, deciduous and coniferous forests, and sweeping meadows that unroll beneath craggy, glaciated peaks. Snow leopards, brown and Asiatic black bear, musk deer, blue sheep and other rare animal species live in this scenically stunning alpine paradise.

Though Govind National Park was established in 1990, nothing changed for the Van Gujjars until 2006. That spring, the forest department in Uttarakhand announced that they might not let Van Gujjars enter the park. After delaying a decision for a couple of weeks, they finally relented and granted "the permission." But in 2007 and 2008, the same situation played out all over again, with increasingly tough rhetoric by the government and rising anxieties for the Van Gujjars, as the authorities kept the nomads of Govind National Park waiting longer and longer each year before allowing them up to their pastures.

In 2009, when I was there, the forest department swore that it was not going to let the buffalo herders into Govind—that year, or ever again. If true, it would be devastating. Dhumman's family and the others weren't simply setting off on a summer holiday to the mountains—they needed to get their herds to the highlands where there was abundant grass and water, or the animals would die and their world would be shattered.

Despite the threats made by the park authorities, Dhumman said he had to try to reach his family's meadow. If there was one force in his life more powerful than the forest department, it was Mother Nature, and she was urging him to get moving. Temperatures in the Shivaliks were already skyrocketing, there was hardly any water anywhere, and the forest foliage was rapidly beginning to fall.

His family would start off, he said, because they had no choice. But he had little confidence that they'd be allowed to access their Himalayan home. And if they couldn't, he didn't know what they were going to do.

❦

By the time dinner was served, the hut was dark. I'd brought several pounds of potatoes and cauliflower to give to my hosts so as not to be a burden on their finances or food supplies, and they'd cooked some of them up in a spicy sauce, which was served in small porcelain bowls and eaten with chapatis fresh off the fire. When I finished, another bowl instantly arrived, and I was counselled by my translator to pour some of it into my original bowl, then leave the rest—showing that I enjoyed the food enough to have more, but not eating too much of the limited amount cooked for the family. Jamila watched closely to see how I would handle the piquancy, and was pleasantly surprised when I told her that where I lived, in New Mexico, many dishes come smothered in spicy chili sauce. She could cook freely without worrying about my taste buds.

When it was time to sleep, I laid down on the camping pad I'd brought, covered myself with my thin blanket, and replayed the day in my mind. I hadn't realized quite how dire the scenario that this family was facing would be. Since they'd always received permission to go to their meadow in the past, I'd assumed that the threats of the forest department would be disregarded as noisy political theatre. But Dhumman was truly anxious; he thought there was a very real possibility that his family would be barred from entering the national park. I wondered how things would unfold once the migration began, and what they would do if the park authorities refused to back down. Selfishly, I couldn't help but wonder how it would affect the story I hoped to tell. If they weren't allowed up to their summer range, would my whole project fall apart? Or might it become a valuable record of one nomadic family's plight, as they and their way of life became victims of heartless government policies? Or would the storyline evolve in some completely unpredictible direction? I couldn't even guess. So, eventually, I stopped thinking about it, and my mind filled instead with images of buffaloes, tree-climbing teenagers, and this little home deep in the forest. I drifted off, feeling incredibly fortunate to have found a door into the world of the Van Gujjars and into the life of this beautiful family—no matter what would happen in the weeks to come.

I left late the next morning, after the milking was done, to head back to Dehradun. When I returned to the forest a week later to begin the migration, it was a sweet kind of reunion, with the warm greetings of seeing friends again. It seemed like we had somehow become closer during the time I was away, that during my absence we came to know each other better than when I had left.

The family was busily preparing for their departure. Dhumman, Mir Hamza, and Sharafat shored up the roof of their hut, adding more grass and tying long vines over its peak and down its sides, securing it against the monsoon rains that were sure to pour down over the summer. Jamila sat outside in the shade, reinforcing the seams of the horsehair saddlebags that would hold the bulk of their belongings during their trek into the Himalayas. Finishing each pair, she gave them to Appa, inside the hut, who packed them with clothing and blankets while keeping an eye on Salma, her five-year-old sister, and Yasin, her round-cheeked two-year-old brother, who ran around barefooted in a perpetually dirty kurta.

Even the buffaloes sensed it was time to go, and were getting impatient to hit the trail. Sharafat told me that the older ones, which had migrated each spring since they were calves, knew the route to the meadow by heart and could make it there on their own, with no human guidance. Sometimes, they even had to be held back from leaving before the family was ready.

Amid the preparations, other Van Gujjars came to the camp to say goodbye. They, too, would be leaving the Shivaliks for the Himalayas, but there was a good chance they wouldn't see Dhumman and his family until they all returned in October, as they spent the summer spread across the mountains of Uttarakhand and Himachal Pradesh. More than just a casual "see you in a few months," there was a ritual element to these farewells.

Sitting in a circle with men and women all together, Dhumman and Jamila and their visitors apologized for any way in which they might have wronged each other, even unknowingly, and asked for forgiveness. Outstanding debts were paid and collected. Words of blessing and goodwill were exchanged. And, in 2009, these gatherings inevitably evolved into conversations about the one thing that was on everyone's mind: whether or not they would be allowed to go to their summer pastures. Nothing had changed since I'd first discussed the situation with Dhumman a week earlier. The forest department had continued to dig in its heels, its threats sounding like promises. The nomads knew they had little control over their fate. They would simply have to start off and see how events played out.

That night, the family went to bed early, knowing they wouldn't have long to sleep. All of their *lathis* were lined up against the wall, right beside the doorway, so they could be grabbed instantly on the way out. The pack animals, which usually roamed freely, were hitched to trees not far from the hut. Everything was as ready as it could be.

We woke in the wee hours past midnight. After Dhumman had finished praying, Jamila had finished packing, Appa had finished brewing tea and churning butter, the boys had loaded the family's belongings on their horses and bulls, and Goku had leashed the dog, it was time to go. Jamila double-checked to make sure they'd remembered everything. She couldn't quite shake the feeling that they were leaving something behind. Later, she laughed at herself, saying, "We hardly own enough to forget anything, but I still worry about it!"

Then, with a jingling of bells, the stamping of a-hundred-and-eighty hooves, and a whole lot of dust in the air, the family set off down the trail in the dark.

2

OVER AND OUT
OF THE HILLS

❧

W hen they reached the confluence with the main *rao*, they were met by one of Dhumman's older brothers, Yusuf, who was waiting there with his family and their buffaloes. Yusuf was lanky like Dhumman, and had similarly chiselled features, but his pointy beard was dyed bright orange, leaping from his chin like a flame. He was the father of Mariam (the tree-climbing warrior-princess), her sister, and her four brothers. His wife, Roshni, had clearly once been a great beauty; she was now beset by the aches and pains earned by a lifetime of hard labor, but still had a sparkle in her eyes and a touch of mischief in her smile. Rounding out the family were two daughters-in-law and six young grandchildren. From this point on, we would all travel together. They fell into a loosely organized formation, with the pack animals in front and the buffaloes in back, moving north, deeper into the Shivaliks.

The streambed was like an avenue paved with white stones rounded by the water that rushes over them during the monsoon. Completely dry now but for a rare landlocked puddle or random trickle that quickly petered out, the *rao* was wide enough to clear a broad, serpentine swath through the jungle. The night sky glittered overhead, casting just enough starlight for this caravan—now eighty-six buffaloes, twenty-six people, two dogs and a handful of pack animals—to travel by.

Before they could work their way into the Himalayas, the families first had to leave the jungle. This involved climbing up and over the Shivalik's steep southern flank, then down its northern slopes and out into the flat, open farmlands near the confluence of the Yamuna and Asan Rivers. This first day's goal was to get as close as possible to Shakumbhari Pass, a gap in the daunting cliffs of the Shivalik's central ridgeline through which they could cross to the other side of the hills.

I carried everything I thought I'd need in a large backpack, including clothes, a sleeping bag, photo gear, a notebook, pens, maps, and hiking shoes for the high mountains. Knowing we'd often be far from towns, I'd brought a first-aid kit, a variety of medications from antacids to antibiotics, and a bag of Nescafe to support my caffeine addiction. I didn't have a laptop, since I saw no real use for one, and was happier without the extra weight, but I did have an old clamshell mobile phone. I wore sandals, lightweight pants, and a short-sleeved shirt.

As dawn lit the hills, the terrain began to rise sharply around the streambed. Soon, we were winding through canyons, sometimes between sheer walls of exposed sedimentary strata, other times below fluted slopes speckled with brown grasses and bare trees. Most of the forest's foliage was already gone. It was a skeletal landscape, stripped down to bony branches and naked earth.

All of the pack horses and most of the bulls wore strings of round metal bells around their necks; with every step they took, each bell chimed in a slightly different way, at a slightly different time. Quickly-changing rhythms and perpetually shifting tones wove in and out of one another, creating a cheery cascade of sound that was mesmerizingly musical. And though the movement of the animals obviously caused the bells to ring, it seemed it was the ringing of the bells that kept the caravan in motion—as though we were propelled forward by a gentle current that couldn't be seen or felt, only heard, and if the bells stopped, so would we.

Every so often, we passed other Van Gujjar camps, some already empty, some still occupied. As we rounded a bend in the canyon bottom where a couple of huts were perched, the nomads living there told Dhumman and Yusuf that we had already passed the last of the water in the drainage. We wouldn't find any more until after we emerged from the Shivaliks.

This was unexpected and unwelcome news. The families had hoped to press on to the base of the pass, but we had to camp within striking distance of a water source. There was no choice but to halt.

The group temporarily split up. Some of us, led by Jamila and Roshni, went a few hundred yards ahead with the pack animals, while the others herded the buffaloes off in search of fodder and shade.

Jamila and Roshni set up their camps in the streambed, in a place where the canyon was about a hundred feet wide and bound on either side by nearly vertical walls of rock and earth that were speckled here and there with bushes and dead-looking trees. There was little flat ground, just a sliver of a bank along the eastern edge of the *rao* and some small spits of dirt that emerged like miniature islands from the water-worn stones. As a result, Jamila and Roshni chose spots about fifty yards apart from each other. The horses and bulls were unloaded, and the saddlebags, water jugs, food sacks and cooking pots were stacked on the ground in an impeccably organized arrangement; I saw that these women kept their temporary camps along the trail in as orderly a manner as they kept the huts at their *deras*. In fact, the word *dera* doesn't just refer to the base camps or the huts in which a Van Gujjar family spends winters and summers. It connotes an idea of "home" and refers to the household itself—the most important parts of which are the people and the animals, rather than any physical structure or geographical place. The *dera* moves with the family—meaning that, on some level, wherever these nomads find themselves, they are home. If they keep their *deras* organized at their seasonal encampments, there's no reason they wouldn't do the same on the trail.

Roshni was accompanied by her daughters Mariam and Khatoon, and her daughters-in-law Fatima and Akloo and their small children. Akloo, who was about twenty-four years old, was striking in her appearance, with dark, almond-shaped eyes and a face that would have been a sculptor's dream. Her strong, perfectly proportioned features conveyed nobility and kindness and a flash of ferocity. She was married to Gamee—Yusuf and Roshni's eldest son—and had two kids—Karim, aged four, and Hasina, who was about eighteen months old. Fatima, who was about twenty-five, was the wife of Chamar—Yusuf and Roshni's second-born son—and was the mother of Rustem (six years old), Djennam Khatoon (three years old), Delai Ka (eighteen months old), and Halima (ten weeks old). Fatima often seemed weary from tending to so many small children, but was an astute observer of—and wry commentator upon—whatever was going on around her. Her husband, Chamar, had dashing good looks, the strength of a demigod, and a boyish, boisterous personality—unlike Gamee, who was more mellow and serious-minded, seeming to embrace the persona of a responsible first-born son.

Jamila had brought Appa, Sharafat, Goku, Salma and Yasin with her, as well as Dhumman's nephew, Mustooq. Mustooq's father, Noor Alam, was deemed too elderly and sick to survive the migration, so Mustooq's wife and two children stayed behind in the Shivaliks to care for him. Mustooq himself would return to them as soon as he had finished helping Dhumman move to the mountains. He was stocky, strong, and experienced, and a great asset on the trail.

While decades ago virtually no Van Gujjar would have spent the summer in the jungles, it's become increasingly common for some—especially the very oldest and most infirm—to remain behind. Most of Noor Alam's buffaloes would go to the Himalayas with Dhumman and Yusuf, but he kept one back, plus a calf, for milk. With little natural fodder remaining around their *dera*, Mustooq said they'd have to bring in grass from a farm on the edge of the Shivaliks, which wasn't cheap, but was doable with only one large and one small mouth to feed. They could only hope that the scant water sources would last until the monsoons hit.

Once the horses and bulls were unloaded, Appa and Sharafat were sent out to the hillsides to find whatever grass they could scrounge and haul it back to the camp, so the buffaloes would have something to eat when Dhumman brought them in that afternoon. Goku and Mustooq took plastic jugs, each with a capacity of about five gallons, to fetch water from the last puddle we'd passed, while I foraged for wood, happy to be doing something useful. Meanwhile, Jamila got busy in the kitchen, making dough, rolling chapatis and cooking them on a pan over a fire; they'd be eaten later, smeared with butter and spicy chili paste.

It was around ten o'clock in the morning, and the heat already pummeled the canyon with crippling force. When Appa and Sharafat returned with small bales of fodder, sweat pouring down their faces, Jamila teased them sarcastically about their skimpy loads. Agitated by exertion and frustrated themselves at their poor harvest, the two were in no mood for jokes; they protested angrily that they'd done their best—there simply wasn't much grass to be found around here. A dose of sweet chai improved their outlook, and they were off again, searching in a different direction.

When Goku and Mustooq returned with water, Jamila filled up a handful of smaller containers, leaving one of the big jugs empty. I volunteered to get more, and Jamila sent little Salma with me, to make sure I wouldn't get lost. As we walked nearly a mile back to the water hole, she chattered away as though I understood every word she was saying. She was spunky and truly adorable, with large dark eyes, rounded cheeks, a winning smile, and a wild nest of hair that was usually pulled back in a braid. When we reached the large puddle, she took the small stainless steel bowl she was carrying, scooped up some water, and poured it into the mouth of the jug, proudly demonstrating what to do as though she was revealing a secret Van Gujjar technique that, as an outsider, I never would have been able to figure out on my own.

The jug fit inside a bag made from an old rice sack, which had a long carrying strap. It was heavy and awkward and, after experimenting with a few different methods of lifting it, I put the strap over the top of my head, with the jug pressing against my lower back, mimicking the way we had hauled huge piles of leaves to Dhumman's *dera* during my first day in the jungle. Since there was no cap, water sloshed all over me as I staggered up the canyon, as graceful as a drunk orangutan. When we reached the *dera* where the other Van Gujjars had told us that there was no more water upstream, they stopped me and explained—using hand gestures—that it would be better to put my head completely through the strap, which should rest on my shoulders. My shoulders would serve as a fulcrum, balancing the weight of the water behind me with the force I would apply by pulling the strap downward in front of my chest. That was the idea, anyway. In reality, the strap cut mercilessly into my shoulders and, with each step I took, the jug slid lower and lower on my back, until the strap pulled back against my throat, threatening to strangle me. I would stop to readjust, then make a couple of minutes of progress, then stop again. Meanwhile, my patient five-year-old friend talked on and on.

Eventually, I got the jug back to camp with most of the water still inside. If I'd had any romantic notions about what it was like to be a nomad on migration, they'd already been dashed. Even this simplest of tasks was a massive effort, and more than a little painful. But I was glad I'd done it. It felt important to immediately establish that I wanted to be as useful as possible, hoping my presence would be more of a benefit to the family than a burden. During the first days of the migration, Dhumman and Jamila grappled with an impulse to discourage me from helping, since they still regarded me as a guest, and guests should not be made to work. But the advantages of a couple of extra willing hands were too great to dismiss.

Later that day, Jamila, laughing, said that the people who had shown me how to carry the jug had been amazed to see an *Angrez* hauling water like that, as though they could not imagine a white person deigning to do such demeaning manual labor. Jamila and Dhumman both took this to be a good thing, though I'm not sure exactly why; they seemed proud that their family's *Angrez* had defied stereotypes to work—even in a small way—like a Van Gujjar.

By early afternoon, the young children wilted and dropped from the heat, passing out in dappled pools of shade. I took shelter under a tree that still had leaves, about a hundred yards from camp. Sharafat, done with collecting grass, joined me. It was simply too hot for anyone to do much of anything.

This teenager had an obviously keen intellect. The previous autumn, Dhumman had been persuaded to take the very unusual step of sending him away to a boarding school in a small village about nine miles from their *dera*. But after a couple of months, Dhumman called his son back to the forest, needing his help with the buffaloes. Sharafat loved school, loved learning, and was deeply disappointed that he'd had to leave it. But neither of his parents, and indeed very few Van Gujjars at all, knew how to read or write, and while Dhumman sensed there'd probably be some abstract kind of value in it if Sharafat was literate, it wasn't deemed important to his success as a buffalo herder. That was little comfort to Sharafat, who said he would much rather go to school than herd buffaloes. But he wasn't about to leave his family and his world and strike out on his own in search of an education. Such a move would be unthinkably radical.

There had been a time about a decade earlier when the non-profit Rural Litigation and Entitlement Kendra (RLEK), which had helped Van Gujjars in their struggle to remain in Rajaji

National Park in the 1990s, sent teachers into the Shivaliks to educate young nomads. Appa had studied in the program, and thrived in it, but it only ran for two years. Ten years later, she could still sound out written Hindi at about a first grade level, making her the best reader in the family. Like her brother, the little taste of education she'd gotten made her crave more—but unlike him, given the choice, she wouldn't have traded her forest-dwelling life for it.

As we sat in the shadow of the tree, Sharafat began to indulge his curiosities. He wanted to know what languages people speak in America, which religions are practiced there, and what kind of food people like to eat. Then he asked if I kept any buffaloes at my home. When I said "no," he asked if I owned cows instead. I said "no" again, and explained that all of the milk that I—and most Americans—use is purchased in containers at a store. "Oh," he said, "Like Amul, India's best-known brand of packaged dairy products. "Exactly."

"But you know," he said with a touch of disdain, "that's not as good as fresh milk."

"Yes, I know," I agreed. I then told him that many Americans prefer to buy milk that has virtually no fat.

"Really??" he exclaimed, skeptically.

"It's true," I said, explaining that the fat was removed before the milk was sold, and that this kind of milk was very popular. As Namith translated, I watched Sharafat's eyes widen. I might as well have told him that only children under the age of ten were allowed to practice medicine. One of the fundamental truths of his world is: the higher the fat content, the better the milk.

This didn't seem like a mere matter of opinion, but like a fact as obvious and irrefutable as "water makes things wet."

After a pause, Sharafat changed the subject completely, asking if I was nervous about tackling Shakumbhari Pass. "No . . . ," I said, ". . . should I be?"

"Well, it's not going to be easy," he said. His family had been warned that the trail was in horrible condition and would be dicey, especially for loaded pack animals. It was even suggested that they wait until daylight to attempt it, so at least they'd be able to see what they were doing. "But, unless my father changes his mind, we're going to try it tonight," Sharafat said. After weighing their options, Dhumman and Yusuf had decided that the daytime heat would be more dangerous for the pack animals than the darkness.

As the sun slid towards the jagged rim of the canyon wall, angular shadows stretched across the bottom of the gorge. Sharafat, Namith and I left the tree and walked over to the kitchen, where Appa was making tea. She smiled, with no trace of shyness or impropriety at being around two men who were not part of the family.

Van Gujjar women are not raised to be demure or subservient. They speak their minds, whether cracking sarcastic jokes or voicing thoughtful opinions; though fathers have the highest status in the family structure, they generally respect what their wives and older daughters have to say. And while Van Gujjar *lambardars* are all male, they consult with and listen to the opinions of the women in the community. In their daily lives, and on the migration, men and women often do the same jobs, from milking and herding buffaloes to lopping and hauling fodder to loading and leading the pack animals. Women generally do the cooking and are the primary caregivers for the young children— but men are demonstratively affectionate with the little ones, too.

Unlike many Muslim cultures in which men may take up to four wives, Van Gujjar men have only one at a time. And a Van Gujjar woman will only veil her face once in her life, for the same reason an American woman will: her wedding ceremony. Well aware of the symbology of the veil—and resoundingly rejecting it—the women have a saying: "Just because you wear a veil for your wedding doesn't mean your husband can tie it around your neck." If the marriage doesn't work out, women can divorce their husbands without bringing shame upon themselves or their family, and without being stigmatized or socially outcast by the tribe.

Appa herself had only recently returned to her family-of-origin after leaving her husband, with whom she was deeply unhappy. He was about eight years younger than she, making him about fourteen years old. "We have nothing in common," she told me. "I can't even talk to him about anything. He's just a boy." Her in-laws, she said, with whom she and her husband had lived, weren't the most pleasant people to share a hut with. She had tried to stay, knowing that would be easier for everybody, but found it unbearable.

Like most Van Gujjar unions, hers had been arranged by her parents as part of a larger marriage deal between families. Since, as a rule, a woman lives with her husband's family, when a daughter leaves her parents, a gaping hole is created in that family's labor force. As a result, marriages are often arranged as exchanges—in its simplest form, a girl from Family A marries into Family B, and a girl from Family B marries into Family A; in Appa's situation, she was promised to a certain boy as part of a more complicated deal, the main goal of which was to get a new wife for one of Dhumman and Yusuf's brothers, who was a widower. Being single, I quickly saw, was not a viable option for Van Gujjars, as the amount of work it takes to survive in the forest is too onerous for one person alone. If you can't maintain your own household, you join a family member's *dera*. The great fear, which motivates and perpetuates the arranged marriage system, is that one's child will be left without a spouse.

Thus it is common for marriage exchanges to involve a complex arithmetic of boys and girls or men and women between two or more families; perhaps a girl from Family A marries a boy from Family B, then a girl from Family B marries a boy from Family C, and a girl from Family C marries a boy from Family A—to give a fairly straightforward example. In order to make some of these arrangements work, it's not unusual for children to be married—though a girl who is married at a young age will stay with her own family until her late teens or early twenties, when she's deemed old enough to leave home.

Love matches, however, are not unheard of. Sometimes when a man or a woman knows that they've been betrothed by their parents to someone with whom they don't want to spend the rest of their lives, he or she may elope with someone else who they find more appealing, before their scheduled wedding day. Such behavior is discouraged since it throws the entire, larger marriage exchange between families into chaos—but it's also understood, and once what's done is done, the illicit marriage is usually accepted by the parents of the bride and groom. The soap-opera-like intrigue around engagements and weddings and elopements and divorces is, naturally, a hot topic for gossip and is one of the Van Gujjars' main diversions; in fact, it seems like the entertainment value of juicy nuptial dramas is as much a reason for maintaining the system of arranged marriages as anything else.

Many arranged marriages encounter substantial turbulence, and it's quite common for women to return to their own families for periods of time. When this happens, the effects often ripple out beyond the troubled couple. In Appa's case, for instance, the wife of her brother, Mir Hamza, was her husband's sister. Since Appa returned to her family, her husband's sister was recalled by her own family to compensate for the loss of labor, and to use as a bargaining chip. So Mir Hamza would have to do without his wife for some time, possibly until Appa officially settled her divorce. Mir Hamza didn't seem to mind.

Unfortunately for Appa, divorces, whether initiated by husband or wife, must be mutually agreed upon, which—in her case—gave her husband the elephant's share of the leverage in negotiating the terms of the divorce. Knowing that she couldn't remarry until the split was finalized, her husband's family demanded an exorbitant sum of money to sign off on it. While negotiations dragged on, Appa was stuck in limbo, unwilling to return to a husband she disliked, yet unable to take a new one and start a family of her own. Dhumman and Jamila both felt terrible about how things worked out for their daughter, and seemed committed to letting her choose her next husband. As soon as she was given the chance.

Appa's husband belonged to one of the families that had been evicted from Rajaji National Park and settled in a village called Gandikhatta, which was built for displaced Van Gujjars by the state government. Since she had gone to live there, she had missed the previous two spring migrations, and was thrilled to be heading up to the mountains once again. Summers in the lowlands were unbearably hot, and "living in the village is like being in prison," she said.

Though marriages are never made outside the tribe, it's not unusual nowadays for matches to be made between nomadic forest families and settled village families. This introduces a whole new set of problems for married couples, especially for the women. When wives move from village to forest, they struggle with the physical demands of wilderness life; village life is simply easier, and a settled woman who is married off to a forest-dwelling husband rarely has the strength or the skills that her new life requires. Aside from feeling, at least for a time, like she's been exiled to a jungle labor camp, she may also feel useless, like she isn't being helpful to her husband's family. Even worse is when her mother-in-law agrees.

On the other hand, when women move from the forest to a village, as Appa did, they often chafe under the constraints of settled life. They have far more freedom in the wilderness, partly by virtue of the equality of the work they do, and partly because living out in the forest gives them a greater sense of autonomy and privacy than is possible in villages, where more people live more closely together and where more conservative religious beliefs have begun to take root among the traditionally liberal Van Gujjars.

Appa was obviously relieved to be back with her family and back in the forest. This was home, and these were the people she loved. Occasionally, however, the cloud of her unresolved divorce overcame her naturally sunny personality, casting her into a place of distress and confusion. She had no idea when she'd be able to get on with her life.

Sitting there in the bottom of the canyon as the heat of the day gradually ebbed, Appa listened raptly when I told her that I had once been married and divorced, when I was not much older than she. She wanted to know what had brought my ex-wife and I together, why we'd split up, and what happened after that. I answered honestly. Though my circumstances were completely unlike hers, since mine was a true love match that had failed, she was intrigued by the story, and took some solace from hearing that life can be much better after divorce, even if the process of ending the relationship is devastatingly painful.

❦

After a night bivouacked in the streambed, sleeping on whatever flat ground wasn't occupied by buffaloes, we were awake by 2 AM. The pack animals were loaded in darkness while chai was brewed on the fire. Soon after we set off, the canyon tightened. Turrets of rock towered above, like Gothic shadows against the moonless sky. Moving through the night, following the twists and turns hewn into the topography, we eventually found the route that cut up and out of the canyon.

The narrow trail was notched into the face of a sheer cliff, as it climbed higher and higher, up towards the spine of the Shivaliks. The path was steep and often treacherous. In one place, we had to scramble about one hundred feet straight up a small landslide. Namith and I were advised to wait until all the animals had made it over this section, then follow, so we wouldn't be caught among the herd, in case any of the buffaloes stumbled or fell. With much shouting to each other and at the animals, the family guided the herd up the chute of loose dirt. Once the way seemed clear, Namith and I started up. We got about halfway when Namith lost his footing and began sliding back down, clawing at the dirt to brake himself.

He managed to prevent himself from peeling off the slope and tumbling to the bottom, but he was clearly shaken. "I don't think I can make it," he said, panting. "I have a heart condition, you know." I didn't know. I told him to stay where he was—I would climb up to where the landslide rejoined the trail, drop my backpack, then return and take his pack, thinking it'd be much easier for him to climb with no weight to carry.

Just as I got to the trail and was removing my pack, Mustooq arrived. In an instant, he was bounding down to Namith with the dexterity of a heavyset goat; he shouldered Namith's backpack and gave him his hand, supporting him step by step to the top of the landslide. Namith was profoundly grateful; I was amazed that, in the frenzy of the moment, anyone had time to think about us, since they were all completely occupied with preventing the animals from plunging over the edge of the cliff as their hooves skated across the loose pebbles that littered the trail. But we had not been forgotten.

At last, with great relief but little celebration, the caravan made it through Shakumbhari Pass and over the range's main ridge. In doing so, we crossed from Uttar Pradesh into Uttarakhand—an invisible borderline that was drawn along the crest of the hills less than nine years earlier, when Uttarakhand (then called Uttaranchal) split off from UP to become its own state. In the moment, this movement between states was meaningless, but it would prove to be of major significance in the days and weeks to come.

Compared with what we had just conquered, the descent down the northern slope was fairly easy. By the time we reached the expanse of forest spread across the base of the hills, the hazy glow of first light filtered through the trees. We paused for a few minutes, readjusting the loads on the pack animals and redistributing the young children who were being carried in shawls. Mustooq gave Namith back his backpack and, to my surprise, Jamila handed me Kutta's leash.

We continued on over flat, well-trodden trails. Here, the arboreal clock appeared to be set a week or two behind the southern side of the ridge; while leaves littered the ground, crunching under foot and hoof, plenty of green still blanketed the branches above. I was happy with my assignment, and recognized its significance: the fact that the dog—who acted like it would have killed me when I first arrived at the *dera*—was now allowing me to handle it, seemed to symbolize that I was no longer a stranger to the family. I'd been accepted even by its most discerning member.

Approaching the edge of the forest, the women gathered firewood, which they would carry atop their heads to the next camp—a few miles away—where they knew they would find none. Dhumman, Yusuf, and a handful of their children stopped for a few hours in one of the last groves of trees, keeping the herd where there was fodder and shade, as Jamila, Roshni, and the rest of the family guided the pack animals on ahead.

Most of the year, whether in the Shivaliks or the Himalayas, Van Gujjars dwell in isolated places out of sight of the rest of the world. They say they live 'behind the veil of the forest," and that is where they are most comfortable. But while they are migrating between the jungles and the mountains, they are exposed, living out in the open within sight of others. When they first leave the paths that run through the Shivaliks, stepping onto a paved road lined with villages and coursing with automobiles, the veil they normally live behind is suddenly lifted.

That moment had arrived.

3

WAITING
BY THE RIVER

I t was like waking abruptly from a dream.

Walking out of the calm of the forest, we suddenly found ourselves in a jarring reality where trucks barrelled past on the road, frighteningly close and frighteningly fast, horns blaring. As we passed through villages, local people came out of their homes to watch the nomadic procession, to see this annual parade of strangers from the other side of the hills. It seemed to me that a subtle self-consciousness settled over the family as the gaze of others first fell upon them, but looking back on that moment, I wonder if I imagined that; if perhaps I was more sensitive to the differences between these Muslim forest dwellers and Hindu villagers than they were. I honestly don't know.

Jamila, Roshni and the rest of us who had been sent ahead with the pack animals followed a narrow road that led to the Asan River. Once we reached the river, we turned left, marching west along the banks, sometimes splashing across the water where it looked most shallow to short-cut the looping meanders. Though the Asan is the main drainage system for the Doon Valley—a basin between the Shivaliks and the Himalayas, within which the city of Dehradun is located—it runs low in April, braiding into channels; in some sections, the water barely reached my ankles, while in others the buffaloes could stand shoulder-deep.

Jamila and Roshni stopped on an empty patch of floodplain that was large enough to hold both families and all of their animals. On one side, we had instant access to the water. On the other, behind an embankment, spread a vast quilt of fields where the buffaloes could graze on the cropped stalks of wheat that had recently been harvested. Perhaps a hundred other Van Gujjar families who'd emerged from the forest over the previous few days were camped along the length of the river, resting their animals before moving towards the Himalayas. Normally dispersed over many square miles of difficult jungle or mountain terrain, here the nomads could easily meet to share news and gossip.

Once the horses and bulls were unloaded, cook fires were started and tea and *khichri* were prepared. There'd been nothing to eat since an early dinner the previous night, long before the climb over Shakumbhari Pass. While the food cooked, each family pitched a shelter made from black plastic sheeting, which was propped up with sticks and secured with rope. Large enough for a whole family to crawl beneath, the tarps were flimsy but effective shields from the brutal assault of the midday sun. Years ago, Van Gujjars carried fabric tents with them, but switched to plastic because it is lighter and cheaper, if not as durable. There were so many tiny punctures in Dhumman's tarp that, when gazing up from underneath it during the day, it looked like the ceiling of a planetarium, pierced with countless constellations; the longer lacerations looked like comets streaking across the night sky.

Dhumman, Yusuf and the rest of those who'd stayed with the herd arrived a couple of hours later. The buffaloes immersed in the river to cool off, while the family ducked under the tents, grateful for shade and tea and food. Dhumman was silent while he ate. I was beginning to see that no time was as sacred as mealtime, in a completely secular kind of way; more than sleep, even more than prayer, it was the one activity during the day that was not to be interrupted.

When he finished, Dhumman said he thought it would be best if we planned on camping here for about a week. I asked him why, and he said that there were two reasons.

The first was something that Van Gujjars have had to reckon with forever: optimizing the timing of their ascent into the mountains based on seasonal conditions. If they reached their summer meadow too early, it would still be covered with snow. But if they lingered too long en route, they would waste money buying fodder that they didn't need and spend more time on the road—which was much more dangerous and less comfortable than being at their home in the mountains. So they moved strategically, aiming to get to their Himalayan pastures as soon as the grass had come up, but not before then.

Now, Dhumman also had to factor in the forest department's refusal to grant him access to his meadow. He hoped that, given a little time, the authorities would relent, as they had during the previous couple of years. Waiting a week along the Asan might mean the difference between moving forward with confidence, or with nerve-wracking uncertainty. And while still in the lowlands, it would be relatively easy to reach forest department headquarters in Dehradun if Yusuf and he needed to appear there in person for any reason.

Dhumman expressed little confidence that the park authorities would change their minds, even if we waited at the Asan for a month. Based on the intensity of their rhetoric, he thought this might be the year that they fulfilled their threats and really kept Govind National Park free of nomads and buffaloes. Dhumman saw no reason why his fate should be any different from that of his many friends and relatives who had once lived in the forests that became Rajaji National Park—and who had been forced out of the wilderness and into a sedentary life. Those evictions had had a seismic impact on the Van Gujjars, personally and culturally, with aftershocks that are still being felt today.

Here's what happened then:

In the autumn of 1992, with little warning, Van Gujjar families that were migrating back down to their traditional winter territiories were blocked by rangers from re-entering the sections of the Shivalik forests that fell within the Rajaji Park boundaries. The nomads, desperate to reach their homes, protested non-violently against the Uttar Pradesh forest department and, with the help of the non-profit Rural Litigation and Entitlement Kendra (RLEK, pronounced "relek"), appealed to the courts.

RLEK was by this time famous for its groundbreaking human rights and environmental victories against powerful, entrenched interests; it had championed a campaign that led to the passage of the Bonded Labor System Abolition Act of 1976, and had filed India's first-ever environmental public interest litigation with the Supreme Court, ultimately forcing the shutdown of over a hundred ecologically damaging limestone quarries around Mussoorie and Dehradun. The director of RLEK, activist Avdhash Kaushal, was alerted to the plight of the Van Gujjars by his son, Praveen, a former pilot in the Indian Navy who worked as a translator for the Swedish anthropologist, Pernille Gooch, when she did her fieldwork among the tribe from 1989 to 1992. Praveen—better known as Manto—would later start SOPHIA, the main organization that currently advocates for the Van Gujjars.

With RLEK on their side, the Van Gujjar families who had been barred from re-entering the Shivaliks in the fall of 1992 quickly secured a temporary stay against their displacement, allowing them full access to their traditional forest lands until their fate could be properly considered.

When the media picked up on the story, the forest department tried to spin the narrative in its favor. They demonized the Van Gujjars as the single greatest threat to the fragile Rajaji ecosystem and portrayed them as the tree-cutting enemies of tigers, elephants, and other wildlife. The nomads, park authorities argued, had to be removed if the forests were to be saved.

Most journalists, however, sided with the tribe. Instead of being depicted as a menace to the forests, Van Gujjars were idealized in print as indigenous environmentalists who loved the forest and knew how to care for it better than anyone, since they had lived in perfect harmony with nature since time immemorial. As a result, much of the public sympathized with the tribe as peace-loving "victims of conservation" who were being abused by callous officials who wanted to push them off their ancestral lands.

The media attention was a mixed blessing. On one hand, it won widespread popular support for the Van Gujjars' cause and gave the government a sense that the public was closely watching the decisions that were being made about the tribe's future. On the other hand, it opened up the Van Gujjars' world to outside eyes for the first time. Before the Rajaji protests, few people knew anything about these secluded buffalo-herding nomads. The media coverage lifted the veil of the forest, and it never quite fell completely back into place.

It was at this time that the tribe began to identify themselves as Van Gujjars. For most of their history, they were known simply as "Gujjars" and only attached the "Van"—meaning "forest"— as a way to distinguish themselves from the millions of other, mostly Hindu, Gujjars in India, with whom they have nothing in common, and with whom they may or may not share distant ancestral roots. Though they are historically related to the goat-herding, Muslim communities of Bakarwal Gujjars who summer in the upper elevations of Kashmir and winter in Jammu or Punjab, the Van Gujjars are a unique and separate tribe. It had never before been important for the Van Gujjars to differentiate themselves from any other Gujjars, since no one paid them any attention, but with the Rajaji Park crisis, they felt it was vital to establish a distinct identity—and to brand themselves as the Gujjars of the Forest.

Looking at the initial efforts to evict the Van Gujjars from Rajaji in the early-to-mid 1990s, it could be argued that the forest department was just doing its job, if heavy-handedly. According to India's Wildlife Protection Act of 1972, when the government decides to create a national park, the first thing it has to do is issue an "initial notification" declaring the proposed boundaries of the park. For Rajaji, that happened in 1983. The next stage is to determine and settle all legitimate claims to that land. Only once that is completed can a park receive its "final notification," after which time virtually all human activity inside the park would be forbidden—except for tourism, research and park management. Grazing livestock within national parks was expressly banned, and people certainly weren't allowed to live in them.

In other words, regardless of how the officials in the forest department felt about the Van Gujjars—even if, hypothetically speaking, they believed that the buffalo herders were beneficial to the forest—by law, they had to get them out—and to settle their claims one way or another—before Rajaji could become a fully-notified national park.

Hence, in 1992, the authorities planned to move the Van Gujjars out of the forest and into a village that had been built for them at a place called Pathri. This would achieve multiple goals: Rajaji would be "freed" from the nomads; the Van Gujjars' claims would be settled through the land compensation scheme; and the forest department could reap substantial amounts of funding for the conservation-based "rehabilitation" of tribal people, offered by the Indian government and international conservation organizations, including the World Wildlife Fund, which didn't want people living in parks.

There were, however, a couple of major flaws with their plan. First, Pathri had been built to accommodate 512 Van Gujjar families, which was the official number that wintered in the Rajaji area, according to the records. But the reality on the ground bore little resemblance to what was on paper, as there were at least three times that number of families in the park. Even if all the homes in Pathri were filled, the majority of the people and livestock would still need to be dealt with.

The bigger obstacle, though, was that the Van Gujjars didn't want to leave the forest. It was their home and they loved it and their life in it. They felt like they belonged there more than in any town. Their buffaloes, they thought, also belonged there, like any other forest animals. Sedentary village life, in a place with no room for their herds, had no appeal to them whatsoever, so they launched a struggle to remain in Rajaji that would last for years.

The nomads were not opposed, in theory, to the preservation of the Rajaji area as a national park. They agreed that it needed protection from development, poaching, logging, and other destructive forces—but not from their buffaloes. In 1996, as the debate over their future was being hotly contested, a group of Van Gujjars collaborated with RLEK to create a plan titled "Community Forest Management in Protected Areas: We will turn this forest into a diamond—A Van Gujjar proposal for the Rajaji Area." It detailed a conservation strategy in which the tribespeople would take the lead in managing Rajaji National Park, with the forest department's role reduced to that of "supporter and monitor." If it had been approved, the Van Gujjars would have been allowed to remain in the park, using their intimate knowledge of the native ecology and geography to maintain and improve the health of the forests—a solution intended to assure "environmental protection while respecting the needs, rights, and traditions of local people."

The plan was heartily endorsed by luminaries such as P.N. Bhagwati, a former chief justice of India, who was vice-chairman of the United Nations Human Rights Commission at the time. He saw in it the possibility to secure "social diversity as well as forest biodiversity." A delegation of Van Gujjars was invited to Delhi to explain and promote their proposal to representatives from the World Bank, which was supporting projects in Indian national parks. But the World Bank and the forest department preferred a more conservative compromise of "joint forest management," which would have given some token jobs to Van Gujjars while leaving the forest department in full control of the park—and still requiring all of the buffalo herders to clear out. According to reports of the meeting, once the World Bank's position became known, one Van Gujjar leader spoke out, saying, "Madam, you call yourself the World Bank, but is it only the forest department that is in the world? Are not we also in this world? Why don't you give us the money and let us take care of the park?"

With their community forest management plan going nowhere, Van Gujjars, again with the aid of RLEK, pleaded their case to stay in the forest to the National Human Rights Commission (NHRC), the Ministry of Tribal Affairs, and the Ministry of Environment and Forests. Between 1998 and 2000, each of these departments issued a series of rulings that, on the surface, were favorable to the tribe, essentially saying that the forest department could not evict the nomads against their will—though the forest department could use "honest means of persuading them to move out." Until Van Gujjar families voluntarily agreed to leave Rajaji, the NHRC declared, "they should not be subjected to any difficulty or harassment by the forest authorities in the enjoyment of their legitimate rights and be allowed to lead their normal life as before," including grazing their herds. Before any family could be moved out of the forest, a district judge was supposed to confirm that they were freely choosing to accept a settlement deal.

Apparently, using "honest means" didn't get the forest department the results it needed. None of the carrots it dangled in front of the Van Gujjars tempted them to leave Rajaji—so, despite the orders against it, park authorities allegedly turned to intimidation, physical violence and outright trickery.

Complaints emerged from the forest of nomads being detained and brutally beaten by rangers; of families being threatened with death if they refused to sign away their rights to stay in the forest; of girls and women being seized and taken from their homes; of buffaloes being confiscated. Some Van Gujjars claimed that they were brought to forest checkpoints, shown pieces of wildlife contraband like tiger skins and ivory, and were then told that if they didn't sign settlement papers, they'd face poaching charges. Sometimes, the authorities allegedly prevented the nomads from performing funeral rituals for their dead. And the rule requiring a judge to certify that each family that moved out of the jungle did so voluntarily was ignored; according to Avdhash Kaushal of RLEK, "corrupt people" in the forest department gave "favors to the judiciary" to turn a blind eye.

All of these accusations were denied by the forest department, which maintained that it had never done anything illegal or unethical in its dealings with the Van Gujjars. You, dear reader, are free to decide who you believe.

The first Van Gujjars to leave the forest were the poorest ones with the smallest herds, who were least able to pay the bribes that the rangers allegedly demanded in exchange for leaving them alone. Many families held out for years, but as the forest department's efforts continued unabated, increasing numbers of Van Gujjars ultimately capitulated. Some say they were driven out of the forest by rampant harassment; others left because they honestly believed the forest department's false promises that they'd be able to get a house in Pathri or the newer, larger settlement at Gandikhatta and still live and graze in Rajaji; others came to sense that this was a hopeless battle that they would never win, so it would be wise to take something while it was being offered, rather than lose everything and get nothing.

Meanwhile, life within the forest was changing. Some Van Gujjar families stopped migrating for fear that if they left the Rajaji area for the summer, they wouldn't be allowed back in. Many other families would leave one or two people behind in the Shivaliks to keep an eye on their huts, for if they were abandoned for five or six months, they'd be destroyed by park rangers. The family would then have to rebuild from scratch, and would have to pay exorbitant bribes to gather the amount of wood they needed for the job (even though they build with dead logs). While most of the buffaloes were still taken up to the high mountains in summer, some herds stayed down low. This put more pressure on the ecosystem than in the past, when seasonal grazing practices gave the forest a chance to fully regenerate in their absence and left the wildlife to use the scant fodder and water sources before the monsoons hit.

The Van Gujjars, of course, recognized this, but there seemed to be a sense that if the forest was going to be taken away from them anyway, they might as well use it while they could. Some started taking leaves from the same trees multiple years in a row, breaking the unwritten Van Gujjar rule that any one tree should only be lopped every other year; some began lopping more aggressively than in the past, leaving far less foliage on the branches, which made it harder for the trees to regenerate.

The park authorities had thus created a self-fulfilling prophecy; by trying to push the Van Gujjars out of Rajaji, the forest department was turning the nomads into the very threats to the environment that it had long claimed they were.

By 2009, most Van Gujjar families had been worn down by what they felt was the forest department's relentless crusade of fear-mongering and abuse, and had agreed to accept settlement in Pathri or Gandikhatta, leaving Rajaji largely empty of nomads—on paper, anyway. As usual, the reality in the forest was different. While many families did clear out of the park, some would leave a few members in the forest with their buffalo herd; this was done in part out of their desire to stay in the forest, but also because, as settlement deals were made with families, older sons who would need independent homes were not counted as eligible for compensation and were denied plots of land within the villages. They had nowhere to go. Other families sent a couple of members to the village, while most of the family remained in the park and paid bribes to the rangers. It was a system that wobbled on a crooked axis, but which had advantages for all: Van Gujjar families were able to keep a foot, and quite a few hooves, inside Rajaji. Rangers were able to continue collecting lucrative payouts from the nomads. Forest department authorities could crow about conservation successes, reporting rapid improvements to the health of wildlife habitats and attributing them to the removal of the Van Gujjars, thus vindicating their displacement strategy—even in areas where nomads still lived.

While accurate figures of how many people remained in the park, even on a part-time basis, are elusive, there are hints. As this book was being finished in 2015, Rajaji, which has still not received its final notification as a national park, was declared India's newest tiger reserve. This has brought new attention to its Van Gujjar residents, who will most likely have to leave the park in the near future, and who will need to be compensated as required by law. According to the forest department, there are 182 families that will need to be settled. According to the Van Gujjars, there are nearly 1,600. SOPHIA, which is working to get an accurate count in order to help facilitate settlement negotiations, estimates the truth is somewhere in the middle, between six hundred and seven hundred families.

On the one hand, it's clear that a significant number of Van Gujjars retained a presence in the park. On the other, it's clear that many left. And, if you believe the stories told by the tribe, it's equally clear that virtually no families went of their own free will. In survey after survey of Van Gujjars—including those conducted by researchers who advocated moving the nomads out of Rajaji—when asked if they would prefer to remain in the park with no interference from the authorities or leave it and settle in a village, literally every single respondent said they would rather stay in the forest.

During the week between my first trip into the Shivaliks and when I returned to embark on the migration, I paid a visit to Gandikhatta, where 878 former forest-dwelling families now live. Instead of camps camouflaged within a rugged jungle, I found homes organized along roads on a flat, open swath of land. Small fields were covered with golden wheat that rippled in the breeze. There was very little livestock. The houses, at first glance, looked similar to traditional Van Gujjar dwellings, but with a couple of profound differences: in the wilderness, the huts have wide doorways, but no doors; at Gandikhatta, the huts not only have doors, they have locks on the doors. And the windows were not large open gaps, but small holes which let in some light but were primarily designed to keep springtime heat out—and when I was there, the day was brutally hot.

I sought out a man named Mullah Noor Alam, who was related to Dhumman through the marriage of one of his sisters. Sitting on charpoys inside his hut, he told me that he had lived in Rajaji National Park. He hadn't wanted to leave, but once the forest department got serious about clearing the forest of nomads, they began physically assaulting Van Gujjars, fining them, and sometimes seizing their buffaloes. Eventually, Mullah Noor Alam decided he had better accept the offer to move to Gandikhatta, or he might get thrown out of Rajaji anyway, and receive nothing.

Once he'd settled in the village, his buffaloes began to get sick. He tried to take them back to the forest, but he couldn't afford the bribes the rangers allegedly demanded of him. He returned to Gandikhatta, where all but one of his animals died from a combination of heat and illness. They hadn't had any shade, he said, since the cattle sheds that a corrupt government-hired contractor had built had fallen down after only a few months, and the Van Gujjars themselves couldn't obtain the materials to rebuild them on their own.

The government, he continued, had been "stepmotherly" in virtually every way that it had built the village, using poor construction materials and techniques. Roofs had blown off in monsoon storms, he said, and since a number of the huts had caught fire, it was decided that it was too risky to supply them with electricity, so they had none.

Whenever Mullah Noor Alam talked about his former life in the forest, his eyes lit up and a smile of fond recognition crossed his face, as though he was thinking of a dear old friend. He still seemed confused about why he and his tribe had been kicked out. "We never harassed the deer or elephants or any other animals," he said. "We would tell the rangers about everything that was going on in the park, so it was harder for the poachers to operate. Now, without us, the forest is less secure, like a house with an open door. Life in the forest used to be great . . ."

But the constant confrontations with the authorities had made it too difficult, he said. Looking on the bright side, he added with just a hint of sour grapes, daily life at Gandikhatta wasn't nearly as strenuous as it had been in the Shivaliks, and his children could go to school, so they had a chance at a better future.

"Sometimes," he told me, with a sparkle returning to his eyes, "I remember the freedom of the forest. Here, we have to be more diplomatic, more careful. In the forest we lived behind a curtain and we could be ourselves . . ." His voice trailed off. "But I've adjusted to this," he continued, "and now that I'm here, I feel I should just accept it and not remember the old life." The light in his eyes dimmed again. Before I left, he said, "You know, to be a Van Gujjar you must keep buffaloes, and live in the forest, and take them to the mountains in summer. We don't do any of this anymore. Soon, we will not be Van Gujjars—we'll just be Gujjars."

Though I hadn't seen enough yet to form an empirical opinion, based on logic alone, I had to agree with his conclusion. If you take away the central element of any culture—in this case, buffaloes—it will undergo radical changes. And Gandikhatta already felt like a completely different world than the one behind the veil—or curtain—of the forest.

I told Dhumman about my experiences at Gandikhatta, and he nodded gravely, saying, "*Ji, ji.*" When I mentioned the fact that the entire time I was there, not one person had offered me any chai, or even any water, he and Jamila, who was listening in, laughed knowingly. "That's a big problem with the settled Gujjars," she said. "They've forgotten the importance of hospitality." There was a hint of pride in her tone, an inflection of satisfaction that the forest Gujjars still knew how to welcome visitors respectably.

As hard as it had been on the Rajaji nomads to leave the wilderness and settle down, Dhumman explained that things could turn out much, much worse for his family and the others who might be banned from Govind National Park. "At least the families in Rajaji were given houses and some land," he said. "We are being offered nothing."

The forest department of Uttarakhand claimed that because the nomads of Govind wintered in the state of Uttar Pradesh, they were not residents of Uttarakhand—thus that state's government had no responsibility for their welfare. The Van Gujjars were depicted as interlopers, as invaders from another state taking advantage of Uttarakhand's precious resources, so Uttarakhand owed them nothing. This argument disregarded the fact that these families spend about the same amount of time in Uttarakhand as in Uttar Pradesh. And the storyline about this nomadic invasion from outside conveniently ignored the reality that Van Gujjar migratory routes and grazing areas hadn't changed in decades or, in many cases, centuries; what *had* changed were the lines on the map of north India, when the state of Uttarakhand was created less than ten years earlier. Before 2000, Dhumman's family spent the entire year within the state of Uttar Pradesh, whether in the jungles or the mountains. How can one invade a place where one has always lived?

"If our meadows are taken and we're not given any compensation, where will we go?" Dhumman asked rhetorically, implying, "nowhere."

In theory, the Van Gujjars of Govind should have had nothing to worry about. In 2006, India passed the Forest Rights Act, which guaranteed the rights of "traditional forest dwellers" to live on and use the lands they have long relied upon for subsistence, even inside national parks. It was a major shift in India's approach to conservation. The only areas from which forest dwellers could be banned were zones designated as 'critical wildlife habitats'— none of which were established in Govind.

The forest department's threat to block migrating families seemed like a blatant violation of the Forest Rights Act but, since Uttarakhand had been slow to implement the law, park authorities completely disregarded it. In fact, its impending implementation seemed to energize them to push the nomads out of Govind while they could cynically argue that they were in a legal gray area, and still operating under the Wildlife Protection Act of 1972.

Despite believing that the law was on his side, Dhumman knew that that might not matter. If the Van Gujjars challenged their eviction in court, the process could take time, and they—and their buffaloes—didn't have much to spare. Besides, he had seen what had happened in Rajaji even after the forest department was forbidden from coercing the herders to leave.

The best thing he could do at the moment, he decided, was to pause for a little while along the Asan River and hope the park authorities were bluffing. In the meantime, he and Yusuf would try to come up with an alternative plan for the summer, in case their nightmare came true.

❧

The days along the Asan River moved to a steady rhythm. The buffaloes were milked in the morning, then moved into nearby fields where they browsed on the stubbly remnants of wheat that had been hand-harvested by farm laborers. Dhumman and Yusuf were usually with the herd, along with a rotating crew of their children, while Jamila and Roshni managed the camp. At midday, the heat battered us with crushing force, surging near 120 degrees. The buffaloes were brought to the river to keep cool while the families sheltered under their tarpaulin covers and dozed off in a stupor. As the sun's fury relented in late afternoon, the animals were taken out to the fields to eat again.

On our first afternoon at the Asan, after the day's cruellest hours had passed, I waded across the knee-deep river with Sharafat to the field where his father and uncle had already led the buffaloes. Rather than steering the animals from pasture to pasture, here the goal was to keep them *in* one place—a plot of land that had recently been gleaned—and *out* of others—the surrounding plots that were still flush with uncut grain, and in which the buffaloes expressed an intense interest.

I'd only gone to see what the herders were doing and spend time around the animals, but within a few minutes Sharafat handed me his *lathi*, then disappeared, thrusting me suddenly from the sidelines into the action. Namith had stayed at the camp, so I looked directly to Dhumman for instructions, which were communicated in hand motions and facial expressions.

Along with Yusuf, Mir Hamza, Gamee, and Bashi, we established a perimeter, and when any of the animals seemed intent on chewing their way into the patches of waist-high wheat outside of their designated grazing area, it was our job to convince them otherwise. For the most part, the buffaloes moved so slowly it hardly looked like they were moving at all—until, as if from nowhere, an entire line of them suddenly seemed about to breach the border. Sometimes a half-hearted wave of a *lathi* was enough to turn them around, while other times we had to dash swiftly to cover gaps in our defenses, shouting and vigorously swinging our sticks. When a buffalo ignored our verbal warnings, a solid whack on its hide would encourage it to turn around. In the field in which they were grazing, there was also a huge heap of threshed wheat piled high in the center, so we had to guard the middle as well as the edges.

It was fun; we were like a team playing zone defense in a weird kind of sport, in which the other team was made up of large, hungry beasts with horns. Though it occurred to me that any of these animals could easily break me in half with a quick lunge of its head, the buffaloes were so generally compliant—like good kids who get caught trying to get away with something they know they shouldn't be doing—that I wasn't afraid of them. Or perhaps I was just being naïve.

As the sun began sliding towards the tilted ridgeline of the Shivalik Range, which sculpted the western and southern horizons, the colors of the sky were washed out in a fog-like haze. We moved the herd in a well-organized, almost single-file formation back to camp, splashing across a shallow section of the river. Coming from the opposite direction, I saw Sharafat and Appa, along with Yusuf's sons Hamju and Chamar, approaching the tents. They were each bent over beneath gargantuan piles of straw-colored grass that towered over their heads and practically engulfed them. It looked like they were being attacked—and swallowed whole—by haystacks. They'd bought the grass from a fodderwala, and had carried their loads for about a mile. All of the grazing, it turned out, was a mere appetizer before the buffaloes' main course. They needed to eat as much as possible to keep their strength up for the journey that, hopefully, lay ahead.

As I sat in the cooking area watching Jamila's hands expertly roll and slap balls of dough into chapatis, Bashi, the eleven-year-old girl, sat down beside me. She told me that I'd done an excellent job out in the field; she had seen that I was watching the buffaloes carefully and had understood what they were doing. I'd be a good herder in no time, she said, adding that she'd personally teach me more the next day. She was so sincere, so visibly pleased with my efforts, that it seemed like, of the two of us, I was the child being praised by my elder.

After dropping their huge loads, Appa and Sharafat came over to join us, brushing grass off their shoulders and out of their hair. They sat with me and Bashi, and Jamila took a break from her chapatis to pour us each some tea. While we drank, Sharafat asked me what got me interested in migrating with them in the first place.

I told them that I had a great love for mountains and deserts, as well as an urge to explore, so when I travelled to foreign countries, I often found myself hiking for days or weeks through remote regions where tourists rarely tread. I had been a wilderness guide in the United States for many years, I explained, so as long as I had my pack, a map, a compass, and a little bit of luck, I could live in and travel through the backcountry quite safely. Often—whether in Mongolia, Morocco, Jordan or elsewhere—the only other people I encountered were nomadic herders, and I was always greeted with great hospitality and plenty of tea. I said I thought that because nomadic people are often strangers in whatever land they are moving through, they have strong traditions of welcoming strangers and opening their homes and tents to them—more so than settled people, who may see strangers as a threat to property that they need to protect. My friends nodded in agreement.

"Maybe I was really drawn to nomadic people," I said, 'because when I'm walking, I'm happy, and when I'm in the wilderness, I'm happy, so I have a natural affinity for nomadic life." The more time I spent with nomads, I continued, the more interested I became in learning about them and writing about them—from their age-old traditions to the ways in which they deal with a world that is changing rapidly around them. And one thing I'd always wanted to do was to experience a migration from start to finish. My friends nodded again. "But why come with us, instead of going with someone else somewhere else?" Appa asked.

In part, I explained, I liked the idea of migrating with people who lived their whole lives in the wilderness rather than with herders who spend half the year or more in towns or villages; plus, I was intrigued by the fact that they had water buffaloes, which to me seemed more interesting than goats, sheep, or cows. But also, I said, very few Americans had heard of the troubles that Van Gujjars or other nomads were having with the establishment of national parks, and it seemed like an important story to tell. "Mmmm, mmmmm," Appa murmured, agreeing. And, I added, trekking up to a meadow in the Himalayas sounded amazing, compared to just about anywhere else I could envision migrating—I imagined it had to be absolutely beautiful. "It is," Sharafat confirmed. "You'll love it up there," said Appa. "It's very, very special."

❧

After dinner, Dhumman, Yusuf, Roshni, and Gamee performed *namaaz*, chanting and prostrating beneath the sparkling night sky. I'd seen scenes like this in many countries I'd travelled to, and guessed that of all the world's religions, Islam probably has the most followers who regularly pray outside.

The form of Islam practiced by Van Gujjars is moderate and tolerant. Prayer regimens are flexible—some days people choose to pray five times, while other days they pray less or not at all. Traditionally, they tend to believe that Allah is just one name among many for God, and that the names that other religions use for the Creator are equally—or almost—as good. They're generally not overly attached to the idea that their conceptions of God, or their ideas of how to worship, are the only legitimate ones—though they do look askance at atheists. When I explained, for example, that I don't pray, but that I connect to something that might be called divine when I spend time in the mountains or the desert, they understood, since for them, God and the natural world are inseparably intertwined. When Namith said he was a complete non-believer, they thought that was strange—but they didn't try to convince him otherwise, and they never proselytized to either of us.

Still, over the last twenty years, and even just over the last three or four, Van Gujjars have grown more religiously conservative. Thanks to the media coverage surrounding the Rajaji conflict, Islamic activists were alerted to the existence of this little-known Muslim tribe living in the hills not far from Dehradun and Haridwar. Preachers went into the forest to teach the Van Gujjars about Islam, and the Van Gujjars, who knew very little about formal religion, met them with open ears, since they wanted to be good Muslims. Once the Rajaji families were settled in villages, they became even easier to reach and to influence. For a time, money flowed in from Middle Eastern countries to build a mosque in Gandikhatta (which, when I visited, hadn't been completed).

In the villages, Van Gujjars were taught passages from the Koran, as well as rules to live by, including the need to eat meat on Bakra Eid (Eid al-Adha)—which repulsed many of these life-long vegetarians, for whom slaughtering animals was abhorrent.

During the few years that I've known them, Dhumman's family has grown noticeably more observant. When I saw them in 2012, Jamila was praying regularly, as were Appa and Sharafat—neither of whom prayed much at all during the 2009 migration. One of the Van Gujjars' core beliefs is that life is primarily driven by destiny or luck—which can easily be understood to mean "written by Allah." Though they're not absolute fatalists and certainly see an important role for human agency, many big events and most end results, good or bad, are viewed as being directed by forces beyond their control.

Like many Muslim communities around the world, Van Gujjars seamlessly blend elements of religious orthodoxy with folk traditions and local superstitions, which I glimpsed for the first time at our Asan camp. Halima, the three-month-old daughter of Chamar and Fatima, was crying constantly and, according to her parents, "didn't seem right." Fatima herself was having trouble producing enough milk for her baby. The couple assumed that an evil spirit was probably involved, so they went to a nearby town, where they paid a visit to a highly regarded holy man. He diagnosed the problem, said the appropriate prayers, and sent mother and daughter away wearing protective amulets, inside of which were bits of paper scrawled with Koranic scripture. Chamar was confident that Halima would feel better soon.

Uniquely among Muslim communities, Van Gujjars see themselves as the spiritual heirs of Esau, eldest son of Isaac and twin brother of Jacob in both the Hebrew Bible and the Koran.

Depending on your interpretation, Esau either sold his birthright or had it stolen from him, and was forced to leave the land of his forefathers. The Van Gujjars have long revered Esau as a saint, and relate to him as one who is outcast—especially, perhaps, as they faced the loss of their own birthright and explusion from the lands of their forefathers.

Hoping to avoid such a fate, Dhumman added some free-style improvisations to the prescribed rituals as he prayed that first night along the Asan. As long as he had Allah's ear, he figured, he might as well ask Him to intervene with the forest department.

In the morning, all of the milk collected from the buffaloes was poured into two containers—one looked like a metal backpack with fabric shoulder straps, the other was a large blue plastic jug with handles at the top. Yusuf's son, Hamju, wore the back-pack, and he and Sharafat each grabbed one of the handles on the plastic jug. I followed as they waded across the river and shuffled up a dirt lane that wended its way between fields and orchards, then through a small village. We emerged on the road that linked Dehradun to Paonta Sahib and waited for a local bus. Luckily, when we boarded, we managed to find enough room to sit at the very back. As the vehicle accelerated and braked and bounced over potholes, I wondered if the containers might be filled with butter by the time we reached Vikasnagar, where Sharafat and Hamju planned on selling the milk. Hamju fiddled with his mobile phone, while Sharafat closed his eyes and rested his head on the window glass.

When we got off the bus, we hustled across Vikasnagar's busy main road, which throbbed with cars, motorcycles, scooters and pedestrians, and was lined with a streetside market and shops of all kinds. My friends knew exactly where they were going, working their way down a side alley. When we got to the milk shop, Hamju and Sharafat immediately asked if they could charge their fathers' mobile phones, and, given a nod of permission, plugged them into the electrical outlets. When in the forest, many Van Gujjars, including Dhumman and Yusuf, lived beyond the reach of mobile connectivity, but on the migration the phones were essential tools, allowing families at different stages of their journeys to share important news with each other and keep in touch with Manto and the SOPHIA staff in Dehradun, who would be the first to know about any developments with the park authorities. Since they couldn't read, they didn't have any names in their "Contacts' lists, but used easily recognizable symbols to represent the people they called most often. Keeping the phones powered up, however, could be a major hassle, requiring trips into villages and hours of waiting for them to recharge.

The dairy shopowner ladled out a small sample of Sharafat and Hamju's milk and fed it into a butyrometer—a bulbed glass tube that looks like something you might have used in high school chemistry class. It was mixed with sulphuric acid and amyl alcohol, then spun in a centrifuge to determine the fat content. After a few minutes, the owner examined the results and offered Sharafat and Hamju twenty-two rupees per liter. It was a fair price back in 2009, and was more than the doodhwala who rode his bicycle into the Shivaliks paid them.

The day was already getting hot, and when we returned to the bustling main road with the empty milk containers, Sharafat and Hamju each bought an ice cream pop. Sharafat explained that he would tell his parents that they'd sold the milk for twenty rupees per liter—a believable number—and that he'd pocket the extra two rupees as baksheesh for his delivery services. I looked at him with an expression of surprise and said, "Really?!" Sharafat, without a trace of guilt, explained that it was all the same, really—if he ever needed something, his parents would end up paying for it one way or another, but this way he wouldn't have to ask them for the money. I laughed at his creative rationalization.

Once, Sharafat continued, he'd been sent to buy a new phone charger for Dhumman, who had broken his. He'd paid about a hundred rupees for it, but told Dhumman it had cost more than twice that—and of course kept the surplus for himself. "But I only did that to save him money in the long run," Sharafat claimed. "I knew if he thought the charger was more expensive, he would take better care of it, so it wouldn't break and need to be replaced as often." I had to admit there was some logic to his reasoning.

Sometimes, like now, he'd spend his money on small treats. But he usually gave it to his sister, Appa, for safekeeping. It's the women, I learned, who generally manage the money in Van Gujjar families, which is one reason why, some say, there is virtually no drinking or gambling in their culture.

Money matters and milk fat percentages seemed to be the only sets of numbers that Van Gujjars spoke of with any degree of precision. For most other things, they would estimate. When I'd first asked Dhumman how many buffaloes he had, he said, "Forty, forty-three . . ." When I asked Sharafat how old he was, he said, "About fifteen, sixteen." He honestly didn't know exactly how long he'd been on the planet, or when his birthday was. Even Chamar and Fatima's tiny baby, who had been born just within the past twelve weeks or so, was "two or three months . . . or maybe three or four months . . . no, two or three months."

Walking past vegetable sellers, I asked Sharafat what he thought his mother would want, and purchased enough eggplant, potatoes, onions and tomatoes to last the family for at least a few days. Since I wasn't paying them any money, I felt it was imperative to contribute amply to our shared food supply.

By the time we got back to the Asan, the buffaloes were wallowing in the water. The people were sprawled out under the tarps, hiding from the sun, napping or chatting with each other. After a few hours, when the heat clicked down a notch from "deadly" to "survivable," the herd was roused from the river and led to a nearby field. I grabbed a *lathi* and went along, eager to get some new tips from Bashi and eventually master the challenge of managing the buffaloes. We stayed until sunset, when we brought the animals back to camp for a full meal of grass that had again been hauled in.

A few vendors walked up and down the banks of the Asan, arms laden with merchandise, drawn by the concentration of potential customers now camped along the river. They were like the hawkers on the beaches of Goa, but instead of sarongs and souvenirs, they carried cookware and rope and livestock bells.

None of them had any luck selling to my companions—until one man flipped the switch on a small LED lantern.

Bright light poured from the little plastic gadget, which he held by its metal handle. Jamila asked to take a closer look, and after some good-natured haggling, bought it. Instantly, the night-time ambience of the camp changed. While the family did have a few flashlights, they used them rarely, for very specific tasks, not to provide light to live by. For that, it was a kerosene lamp and the cook fire—both of which gave off a warm, cozy kind of light, a light that seems alive as it dances or sputters or flares, a light that creates a mood both rustic and romantic. For those of us fortunate enough to live with electricity, the glow cast by flames triggers a trans-generational sense-memory, as though some-where in the back of our brains we can almost remember—and feel a nostalgia for—the firelight that lit our ancestors' worlds for tens of thousands of years. It feels soulful, natural, of the earth.

By contrast, the new lantern emitted a harsh, bluish-white light that was unmistakably artificial. It was like a beam straight out of the modern world, which shattered the magical aura of the fire at night. But it was incredibly practical, and the family embraced it as something that could make their lives easier, expressing no regrets over the change. I may have been the only one to sense the loss that came with the gain.

That evening, Namith told me he didn't see any point in staying on the banks of the Asan, enduring the blistering heat, for days on end. If we walked up to the road and caught a bus, he said, we could be in Dehradun in less than two hours, where there were showers and toilets and electric fans. Dhumman could call and let us know when the family was getting ready to move again, and we could come back and join them then.

This idea had no appeal to me whatsoever. My entire purpose was to participate in the migration from start to finish, whatever that looked like. Barring a medical emergency, I wasn't going to leave. Besides, it's not like it would be any cooler in Dehradun—it would just be dirtier, noisier, and more crowded. But Namith had made up his mind. He was going to leave the next day, he said, regardless of what I wanted to do.

This posed a dilemma for me, since in so many ways I relied on him to be my ears and my voice when talking with the Van Gujjars. I had to question how much I could learn and understand, how well-spent my time would be, without him. After a few minutes of contemplation, I decided to stay, even if I would be communicationally challenged. It turned out to be one of the best decisions I made during the entire journey.

On one hand, the family saw that I was wholeheartedly committed to the migration, and to them. Also, as Namith and I talked about the plan with Dhumman and Jamila, they understood that I was honestly happier to be camped alongside a river with a herd of buffaloes than I would have been back in a busy city; in other words, in at least one important way, I was like them. We had something fundamental in common, and this recognition helped establish a deeper connection between us. Additionally, when Namith left the next day, it gave me an opportunity to interact directly with my companions, rather than through an intermediary. Despite the language barrier, the most essential elements of our personalities shone through in our facial expressions, our postures, and our laughter, and we became closer.

Over the next several days, we settled into a comfortable camaraderie. The unusual reality of an American living alongside the Asan River with a family of nomadic water buffalo herders began to feel perfectly normal, to them and to me.

One morning while I was out grazing the herd with half of the family, I was invited to drink milk directly from a buffalo's udder, as Van Gujjars of all ages often do. It seemed like part initiation ritual and part joke, as the group of young people who were urging me to drink with them awaited my response with suppressed giggles. They were well aware that this wasn't a typical *Angrez* custom. I shrugged and knelt in front of the animal's right rear leg, opened my mouth, gripped a teat in my hand, and squeezed. Nothing came out. My friends burst out laughing. Apparently, the only thing funnier than an American drinking from a buffalo teat was an American who couldn't even get milk to come out of one. Mir Hamza then knelt beside me, grabbed a teat in his hand, angled it toward my face, and stream of warm milk shot into my mouth. After a few good squirts, I stood up and wiped my lips. *"Bohut acha!"* I exclaimed, practicing my fledgling Hindi, and everyone laughed again.

Later, when we took refuge under the tarp and I was showing the teenagers and twenty-something-year-olds the photos I'd taken that morning, Sharafat asked me to videotape him for the first time. As soon as my camera was out, he draped a cloth over his head like a scarf, and launched into a melodramatic monologue in which he pretended to be a heartsick woman, distressed and crying over the loss of her lover. It was so surprising, and so funny, that his brother and sisters and cousins rocked with laughter—and even Jamila, who was trying to maintain her composure, couldn't help but join in.

Of the family elders, she was the most tolerant of and intrigued by the camera. Dhumman, Yusuf and Roshni were wary of the device, concerned that it would have some negative effect on the younger generation. They didn't mind me taking pictures or shooting video; they only seemed to get a bit uncomfortable when their children would gather around to see the images on the back of the camera—as though this kind of entertainment would somehow be a corrupting influence. It was hard to tell whether they had reservations about introducing this kind of technology to their world, or if they just saw it as a distraction from other, more important, tasks.

The kids, however, had no hesitation about the camera. They loved it. One night, Mir Hamza, Chamar, and Hamju, illuminated by a flashlight, crouched on the ground and sang a series of traditional Van Gujjar songs that they wanted me to record on video. Songs are the Van Gujjars' main art form; the women do some needlepoint work, but theirs is not a culture rich in theatre or painting or handicrafts. "We're too busy for those kinds of things," Jamila told me. But they can sing while they herd, while they milk, while they lop leaves or gather firewood. Some of their songs are about love, some are about migrating, some are about buffaloes. Many describe the hardships of their lives with touching poignancy, like poetic pastoralist blues, expressing philosophical thoughts about luck and destiny, life and death, and what it feels like to wonder if you've been forgotten by God.

The three guys sang in a flowing rhythm, hands cupped around their ears, ending each line with a lingering tremolo that gradually faded to silence before the next line began. When they finished, they and their brothers and sisters and cousins crowded around to watch their performances, again and again, until they sensed the disapproving vibe from their parents and decided it was time to go to bed.

The days that follwed were much like the others, herding, resting, and herding again.

After a week had passed, the forest department showed no sign of weakening its resolve to keep the Van Gujjars out of Govind National Park. Dhumman and Yusuf had still not been able to get their grazing permits. But they decided to move closer to the mountains anyway, hoping that by the time they reached their meadows a few weeks later, they would be allowed in.

We left one night, crossing the river at 2:40 AM I carried little Yasin over the water, and paused with the rest of caravan on an island between two channels, as the load on one of the bullocks had to be readjusted. While we waited, Goku came over and offered to take Yasin from me. He clambered out of my arms and perched himself on one of his sister's shoulders, with one leg in front of her, one leg behind her, and his hands atop her head.

Salma stood beside me, sleepily holding the dog's leash. But she woke up quickly: without warning, the bull with the off-balance load went wild, kicking and bucking—then it charged straight at us. Salma screamed and tried to run, but she didn't know where to go and got the leash wrapped around the dog, which started barking and spinning in circles. I reached down, grabbed Salma, and swept her up. She threw her arms around my neck and I held her tightly in one arm, while taking the dog's leash from her with my free hand. But there was no time to get out of the bull's way.

An instant before it would have crushed us, somebody with a lathi leapt in front of it, and somebody else grabbed it by the rope that hung around its neck, turning it away from Salma and me. In a matter of moments, the animal was stilled, and acted as though nothing unusual had happened. The night had gone from calm to total pandemonium back to calm in less than a minute.

Salma, deeply rattled, didn't want to let go of me. I carried her the rest of the way across the river and up to the road. There, she got down. She'd wait with Jamila and Roshni and the other small children for a bus that would drop them near our next planned campsite. The rest of us marched on with the animals, through sleeping villages and past farmers' fields, until we reached the Yamuna River. As the sun crested over the mountains to the east, the first rays of morning spilled down into the valley, where they mixed with thick plumes of dust kicked up by the herd and engulfed us in a cloud of brassy light.

4

UNDER ARREST

W e stopped along the Yamuna River outside the town of Kalsi—a major nexus of Van Gujjar migratory routes, where families from across the Shivaliks had converged. It was hard to gauge exactly how many people were camped there, but it was easily over a thousand. Some, like mine, would head upriver into Uttarakhand's Garhwal Himalayas, while others would cross the bridge and move towards the neighboring state of Himachal Pradesh. Cradled by the foothills yet open to the plains, this was the gateway to the high country.

Unlike at the Asan River, where there was plenty of space between Van Gujjar camps, here families set their tents close together, leaving some open areas for their animals to share. It felt like a festival, the air abuzz with the noises of conversation and commerce, shouting and laughter. With few nearby fields in which to graze, enormous bales of grass were bought out of the backs of cargo trucks for morning and evening feedings. As the day grew violently hot, the buffaloes spent most of their time lounging in the water. I tried to keep as cool as possible myself, resting with Dhumman, Yusuf, and a few other Van Gujjars under a large shade tree by an irrigation ditch. By afternoon, Namith had arrived by bus from Dehradun.

At some point during the day, Dhumman got a call from Manto. SOPHIA was organizing a meeting of Van Gujjars at forest department headquarters in Dehradun the following day, to plead their case with the park officials. Manto knew Dhumman would want to be there, both as someone personally affected by the threatened closure of Govind and as a *lambardar*. A couple of cars would be sent to Kalsi the next morning, Manto said, and Dhumman agreed to round up a handful of others to bring along. When I spoke to Manto later, he asked me to accompany Dhumman so I could take pictures of the meeting, which SOPHIA might be able to use some day. I was curious to see what would happen there, and was happy to have an excuse to go.

Early in the morning, while the sky was still a wash of soft pastels, Dhumman, Yusuf, Namith (who had rejoined us the previous afternoon), and I left our camp and walked to the nearby road, where two faded white Ambassadors were waiting. I met a handful of other Van Gujjars, including Dhumman and Yusuf's cousin, Alfa. A man of regal demeanor, he had arctic-blue eyes that added a startling intensity to his appearance. He was also a *lambardar* heading for Govind, and I would soon come to know him much better. In each car, three people squeezed into the front with the driver, while four of us sat pressed together in the rear. As strange as this scenario could have seemed—five bearded nomads, one local driver, one ethnic Bengali, and an American, tightly packed into a vehicle speeding through the dawn—in the moment it felt perfectly normal.

The forest department campus was a calm and shady oasis off a dusty, traffic-filled commercial street that was lined with grain wholesalers, charcoal dealers, used-auto-parts shops and wedding tent rental agencies. A few modest buildings surrounded a parking lot, on one side of which was a low cement wall that framed in a garden in which leafy trees were planted. The trunks of the young saplings were ringed with wire fencing.

By the time we arrived, some seventy Van Gujjars were already there. They stood around talking, sat on the retaining wall or squatted under the shade trees. Some had interrupted their migrations along various different routes and made their way to Dehradun, while others came from Gandikhatta to lend their support. I was greeted warmly by Manto and the other SOPHIA staffers, but they had work to do, so I settled in near Yusuf, among the nomads, on the periphery of the action.

A prominent leader of Uttarakhand's Congress Party, Suryakant Dhasmana, arrived to voice support for the Van Gujjars and to help negotiate on their behalf with the park authorities. Local journalists came to cover the story, and a handful of Van Gujjars formed a circle around them, not wanting to miss a word as they interviewed Dhasmana, Manto, and Alfa, who was nominated as the spokesperson for the nomads.

To call this event a rally or a protest would be an exaggeration. There were no slogans chanted, no fists or voices raised, no signs or banners waved around. The men and women who had come to speak up for their rights sat peacefully in the shade, talking quietly among themselves, chewing tobacco and smoking *bidis*, by their presence alone showing that they supported the families who needed to access the meadows of Govind. When a small group of *lambardars*—including Dhumman and Alfa—went into the forest office to speak to Rajaji Park Director S.S. Rasaily—who was also in charge of Govind—some of their fellow tribespeople followed as far as the building's porch. They waited under the awning in a hushed state of suspense. A few tried to peer through the windows to glimpse what was going on inside, but most sat patiently, mentally preparing themselves for whatever the news would be when the door opened. They seemed less like a group of people fighting for a political cause and more like a family in a hospital waiting room, wondering whether the surgeons in the operating theatre were going to emerge with a verdict of life or death for an injured loved one.

❦

Ever since the modern environmental movement began in the mid-nineteenth century, "no people in parks" has been a mantra embraced by conservationists and governments worldwide. As national parks, wildlife sanctuaries, and other types of nature reserves have been established around the globe, millions of indigenous people have been forced off of the lands that their tribes had lived on for hundreds if not thousands of years. On the surface, the rationale behind these evictions seems simple: the best way to preserve fragile ecosystems is to keep people— except for tourists—out of them. The reality, however, is much more complex, and always has been.

The vast majority of conservation displacement in recent decades has taken place in Africa and Asia, but the practice was first pioneered in the United States over 140 years ago. In the 1800s, as people of European ancestry spread westward across the Great Plains and the Rocky Mountains all the way to the Pacific coast—drawn by gold or land or religion or adventure or the limitless possibilities of the frontier—certain places of awe-inspiring beauty came to achieve iconic reputations in the American imagination. Among them was the Yellowstone Plateau, where abundant wildlife roams a scenic wonderland of verdant meadows and expansive evergreen forests, where rivers course through dramatic canyons and plunge over sublime waterfalls, where high rocky peaks tower over bizarre geothermal features. Two-thirds of the world's geysers are found there— including the biggest (Steamboat) and the most famous (Old Faithful)—along with searing hot mineral springs and cauldrons of boiling, bubbling mud.

By the time the first awe-struck reports and otherworldly illustrations of Yellowstone emerged, industrialization was rapidly expanding in the eastern part of the country and the wild landscapes of the west were being tamed and fenced and settled. As Americans witnessed the depletion of what had once seemed like a vast, inexhaustible wilderness, a collective sense of nostalgia, mixed with alarm, emerged for what was being lost. Americans rallied around the idea of protecting Yellowstone, and when it became the world's first national park in 1872, the idea was to preserve it in as pristine and natural a state as possible.

Yellowstone and other extraordinary places—such as California's Yosemite Valley—became symbols of the purity of nature and the perfection of God's original creation. Like the Garden of Eden before the arrival of Adam and Eve, they were seen as being free from human influence, places where plants and animals lived and thrived in harmony, away from the meddling, inherently destructive hands of men. As appealing as that sounds, it was a fantasy that bore little resemblance to forces that truly shaped the reality on the ground in the American West.

Native Americans had lived in the Yellowstone area for thousands of years. In the mid-nineteenth century, one clan, called the Sheepeaters, resided there year-round, while other tribes—mainly the Shoshone, Bannock, and Crow—hunted and gathered and camped there on a seasonal basis. They didn't simply shoot a few animals while passing through, but—as humans are inclined to do—actively engineered the Yellowstone ecosystem to meet their needs. They set fires to clear thick underbrush and to open up forested areas, encouraging the expansion of grasslands that could support the populations of deer, elk, bison, and antelope that they hunted. They created a network of trails that they and the wildlife could use to get around. They promoted the growth of the shrubs, berry bushes, and tubers that they valued as food sources, while eliminating competing plant species. In many ways, Yellowstone's environment was, for centuries, tended and cultivated like an actual garden, not one out of Judeo-Christian mythology.

Conservationists in the mid-1800s, however, were blinded in one eye by their visions of pure nature and in the other by their disregard for native peoples. As a result, they had little appreciation for just how profound the human influence on Yellowstone's ecosystem had been. Lacking this understanding, they worried that warriors on horseback might hunt the large game animals to extinction or that the tribes might accidentally burn down the whole forest. They believed that the only way to create the park they imagined was to completely ban Native Americans from it.

Yellowstone had always been important to the tribes, and at the time the park was created it had become absolutely essential to them. Years earlier, when the Shoshone, Bannock, and Crow were forced to live on reservations, the treaties they signed gave them the right to go off their reservations to hunt on public lands. But as white settlers began moving west in greater and greater numbers, the newcomers claimed vast tracts that had once been common property. Overhunting and overgrazing wherever they went, they killed off or drove out the animals that the tribes relied on for survival. Yellowstone Park, however, was off limits, and became a rare haven for wildlife—as well as the largest intact piece of public land in the region.

The tribes knew that park officials didn't want them there, but they now had nowhere else to hunt. And they believed they shouldn't have had to go anywhere else, since their rights to access Yellowstone had, in fact, been guaranteed by the government. Having already ceded most of their ancestral territory, they weren't going to stop harvesting game in the park just because white men now wanted to take that from them, too. In the end, the U.S. Army was called in to chase the tribes out.

Protecting wildlife was only one of the motives for expelling Native Americans from Yellowstone. Administrators also wanted to make the park easily accessible to visitors, but they believed that tourists would stay away if they knew that Native Americans—who were popularly depicted as brutal savages—were roaming freely around there.

Besides, the authorities reasoned, by keeping the tribes on their reservations and forcing them to abandon their so-called "primitive" ways, they might one day become civilized and be able to participate in mainstream American society; banning them from the park, therefore, was for their own good.

As increasing numbers of people toured Yellowstone, along with the other national parks that were created soon after it—from which tribes had also been pushed out—the notion of wilderness as a purely natural place, free of human influence, became cemented in American consciousness. After all, when you visit a park, that's what you see—pure nature, inhabited by no one. The idea had shaped the reality, which confirmed the idea.

Today, over three million people go to Yellowstone each year to experience its wonders. Most have no idea that Native Americans were once forcibly evicted from the park. Few would even imagine that to be the case—since it is pristine wilderness, it logically follows that no one ever lived there.

From a conservation perspective, Yellowstone has largely been a triumph, protecting majestic scenery, important ecosystems, and plant and animal species from the depredations of development. As the conservation movement gradually spread throughout the world, nearly all parks and wildlife reserves were based on the so-called "Yellowstone model." In developing nations, most places worthy of protection—from grassy savannahs, to thick jungles, to alpine meadows, to picturesque deserts—also happened to be inhabited by indigenous or tribal communities whose livelihoods and age-old cultural practices relied on, and were inseparable from, the lands selected for parkdom. Apparently, they never got the message that people don't live in the wilderness. They would have to be moved elsewhere.

Today, over twelve percent of the land on earth has been officially protected. No one knows exactly how many people have been displaced by parks worldwide, but estimates by human rights organizations range from at least five million to tens of millions. Some studies place the number of these so-called "conservation refugees" in Africa alone at around 14 million. In India, since the Wildlife Protection Act of 1972 banned people from parks, the number of *adivasis* and other forest dwellers who have lost their traditional lands is estimated to be somewhere between 100,000 and 1.6 million, while another 3 to 4 million are slated for eviction. Thanks to the passage of the Forest Rights Act, they might now be allowed to remain.

Despite the assurances made by many different governments that taking people out of the wilderness would improve their lives, many conservation refugees have struggled to adjust to lifestyles that they don't want, wallowing in poverty as they've been stripped of the ability to sustain themselves in the only ways they've ever known. Meanwhile, cultural losses have reached tragic proportions, as communities disconnected from their lands and their ways of life, and exposed to new and different influences, simply can't maintain many of their cherished traditions.

In recent years, the human and cultural costs of displacement have begun to be recognized. Some conservationists are stepping away from a strict "no people in parks" mentality, and peoples threatened with eviction have become increasingly empowered to speak up and be heard. In addition to raising provocative human rights issues, many conservation refugees—including the Van Gujjars—make an impassioned environmental case for staying on their traditional lands. They agree that wildlife habitat needs to be protected—they just don't think it needs to be protected from them.

They point out that it's their traditional territory that's been deemed special enough, pristine enough, and home to enough rare wildlife to be worthy of becoming parkland—which, they conclude, means they must be doing something right.

Some of these communities deliberately design their practices to keep their environments in balance, based on an empirical understanding of natural causes and effects. Others have eco-sustainable rules and taboos built into their religious beliefs and superstitions: some pastoralists in the Malian Sahara, for example, never camp in exactly the same place twice, they say, because once they leave, those spots become haunted by evil spirits; this, of course, also happens to give the land a chance to recover after it's been used. Many forest-dwelling people in India maintain sacred groves of trees, dedicated to the gods, which are never cut and remain a rich source of biodiversity. The Maasai, in East Africa, virtually never hunt wildlife for food—though they are surrounded by it—out of a sense of personal pride and peer pressure: "If you have to hunt, it means you are a terrible herder," a Maasai chief from Kenya once told me. In parts of the world where resources are scarce, agreements are often made within and between tribes that establish who can graze, hunt, or harvest at which times and in which places, to avoid overuse and avert conflicts.

Strict environmentalists counter that indigenous people have never been ecological altruists and are not really interested in protecting biodiversity. Rather, their ways of life encourage the continued survival of the plant and animals species that they rely on; other species may happen to benefit indirectly from those practices, while others may suffer or be lost.

At the heart of this debate is a fundamental difference in perspective about the relationship between man and the environment. Many forest-dwelling and indigenous peoples see themselves as integral elements of the natural ecosystems they live within. In other words, they belong there, just like the wildlife does. But most mainstream conservationists disagree: since the forest dwellers are human, they are by definition an invasive species in their ecosystems.

This is the fundamental premise behind the "no-people-in-parks" protocols: that humans cannot be natural, native parts of environmental ecosystems.

While conservationists have long treated this premise as fact, indigenous activists argue that it's simply a theory rooted in deeply entrenched Western biases. The notion of a split between nature and mankind seems like an obvious truth to most Europeans and Americans, the activists contend, because it is based on a set of assumptions that is seamlessly, invisibly ingrained into the conceptual architecture upon which the Western world-view is built. You might attribute the origins of these core assumptions to the teachings of the Catholic Church, or to the philosophy of Descartes, or to an innate Western mentality; whatever their source, the understanding of man's relationship to nature that is drawn from them is not a picture of objective reality, but a culturally-filtered interpretation. As we have seen with the way that Yellowstone has reinforced the idea of pure nature as a place without people, these kinds of assumptions and interpretations can become self-perpetuating and self-validating, to the point that it seems absurd to question them.

Since those who drive and fund the conservation agenda— including large NGOs, the World Bank, and the International Monetary Fund—are mainly based in the U.S. and Europe, when they implement plans that they're convinced are best for the environment, those plans generally reflect their Western belief that humankind is not a part of the natural world. This has led to accusations from conservation refugees that "no people in parks" is a form of "green imperialism."

To them, the idea that forest dwellers are invasive species makes no sense. They've inhabited their lands for so long, they say, that removing them would alter the ecology more than leaving them where they are.

When I was in Kenya, I visited Maasai Mara National Reserve, which is best-known as the home of one of nature's greatest spectacles: the massive wildebeest migration that thunders through each summer and early fall. The Maasai tribespeople who once roamed the savannahs there with their cattle, sheep, and goats were banned from the park and now live around the edges of it. Some still take their herds into the protected area to graze, but only at night, and they don't penetrate very deeply. A local Maasai man told me that the main reason why they were cleared from the park was for tourist appeal. "People come from all over the world to see lions and elephants. They don't want to pay a lot of money to see cows." As long as the grazing was done after dark, when the tourists wouldn't notice, he reasoned, it was okay. According to him, the rangers agreed, and simply looked the other way.

Talking later with a Maasai chief and a biologist, I asked if they had seen any ecological effects within the Maasai Mara that they attributed to the expulsion of the Maasai. Both agreed that the foraging patterns of the wildlife had changed. Before the Maasai were evicted, the wildlife had been more widely dispersed over a greater area, they said. Now, grazing animals—such as gazelles, zebras and topi—are spending more time closer to the fringes of the park, and even outside the park boundaries, in the very areas where the Maasai keep their herds. "Due to the livestock, the grasses there are shorter, so the animals feel safer.

It's harder for lions or cheetahs or leopards to sneak up on them," I was told. Removing the Maasai from their ecosystem had been like pulling on one thread of a tapestry, which then pulls others along with it.

Van Gujjars see themselves as similarly woven into the fabric of their forest world—though with one very unique difference. While the Maasai think of their livestock as domesticated animals, Van Gujjars think of their buffaloes as "jungle animals," little different from other wildlife. In fact, the breed of buffalo that Van Gujjars keep is genetically very close to the breed of wild buffalo that once roamed the Shivaliks, and has substantially different characteristics from the domesticated buffaloes raised elsewhere around India; not only do they thrive in the forest, they are able to climb into the Himalayas. When I showed a Maldhari tribesman from Gujarat photos of Van Gujjar buffaloes migrating into the mountains, he was astonished. "Our buffaloes could never do that," he pronounced. "They would die."

One reason why Van Gujjars don't kill predators such as leopards or tigers is that their buffaloes are quite good at defending themselves. But another reason is that, since the herds are thought of as wildlife themselves, Van Gujjars understand that it's only natural for leopards and tigers to eat them. Though the loss of any buffalo deeply saddens the family that owns it, they don't blame the predator, but accept it as fate, as the way of the forest. And Van Gujjars have deep empathy for the forest creatures. "The animal [in the forest] is seen through the eyes of the lover," one Van Gujjar song goes. "He understands that his life and my life are the same."

In recent years, a growing number of conservationists have come to see the value in the indigenous point of view. They agree that, on the whole, indigenous people have done a pretty good job of living in nature without destroying it, whatever their motives may be. They're open to the possibility of creating protected areas in which people can stay on their traditional lands—partly because they factor the ethics of eviction into their arithmetic, partly because they've come to appreciate the vast amount of knowledge that indigenous cultures have about the ecosystems in which they live, and partly because they reckon it'll actually be better for the environment if people remain within it, where they are a deterrent to poachers and where they'll continue to have a very personal reason to care for the land.

The reason, of course, that these cultures tend to live sustainably is because they know that they're going to be relying on the environment and its plant and animal communities for their own survival, year after year, generation after generation. As a result, they're willing to harvest, graze, or hunt less than they otherwise might, to make sure there is enough for the future, the way Van Gujjars traditionally prune trees in a way that they'll be sure to regenerate.

When faced with eviction, this equation is fundamentally altered. Suddenly, there is no future. It makes sense to take much more from the land than usual, since it's now or never, and if the balance of the ecosystem is thrown off they won't be there to feel it. This is what happened in some parts of Rajaji when the Van Gujjars felt sure they were going to be kicked out of the forest. And I've seen it happen in other places, too.

In 2011, I spent some time in Jordan, around the village of Dana—a tiny settlement of stone houses perched on the edge of a dramatic canyon that plunges about five thousand feet in elevation, through four different climatic zones. For over five hundred years, the Bedouin of the Al Ata'ta tribe used the village as a home base during the summer months; in winter they would descend into the warmer, lower elevations of the canyon system to graze their herds of goats, sheep and camels.

In 1993, the Dana Biosphere Reserve was created, covering about 125 square miles around the village and including much of the land on which the Al Ata'ta relied for grazing.

When I met Hamed Abu Saygir, a Bedouin park ranger who was one of the few shepherds who'd gotten a good job in the nature reserve, I expected him to rave about the success of the conservation efforts in Dana. Instead, he confessed that the land had been healthier when people had lived and grazed their animals on it. Sheep and goats, he said, used to eat the weeds that took over other, slower-growing types of plants, including wild herbs and pistachios. They also devoured insects that infested and killed trees. Since the grazing had stopped, the plant life wasn't as robust or diverse as it had been. But perhaps the biggest impact had come from the change in local people's attitudes about the environment.

In the old days, he said, there was a strict taboo against killing trees. "We wanted the trees to live," he explained. "This is the desert, and we needed their shade for ourselves and our animals. Even if we needed wood, we would never take down a whole tree." Now that families hadn't lived in the reserve for nearly twenty years, the fate of the trees didn't concern them much. Wood poaching in the park was a serious problem, with trunks cut down to stumps, depleting the delicate high desert ecosystem. "We have forgotten that trees are a gift from Allah," Hamed said.

Hamed was not alone; every single person I talked to said that the environment (not to mention the herding families) had suffered since the shepherds had been shut out.

Still, despite the degradation that had occurred, it was better that the area had been turned into a park than left completely unprotected, said Khalid Khawaldeh, another local Bedouin. Otherwise, much of it would have been destroyed by mining companies. It just would have been best, he maintained, if the shepherds were allowed to access the land within the reserve as they had for centuries past, rather than being oppressed by it. Due to the loss of their traditional grazing rights, many families had had to abandon herding altogether; those who kept their herds grappled daily with poverty and stress.

Of course, even if it's accepted that forest-dwelling people have long lived sustainably on their ancestral lands, it's legitimate— and important—to ask whether they still can, today and into the future. Though no fault of their own, the modern world around them is weighing so heavily on the environment that their traditional ways of living, which were once easily absorbed by natural ecosystems, might now be the feather on the scales that knocks these ecosystems out of balance. In other words, due to the impact of climate change, industrial and agricultural encroachment, mineral extraction, legal and illegal logging, poaching, global population growth, urban sprawl, a shrinking base of natural resources, and other factors far beyond the control of indigenous people, it's possible that some age-old techniques of living on the land that were once sustainable no longer are, or will lead to the extinction of some species. As habitat has disappeared, as tribal communities and wildlife are restricted to smaller—sometimes island-like—areas of wilderness, can people who have been living in harmony with nature for hundreds or thousands of years continue to do so? Might their presence crash—or help preserve—the ecosystems they rely on for survival?

These questions can really only be answered on a case-by-case basis, depending on local environmental conditions as well as the specific ways of life of any particular group of people.

The Van Gujjars who spend summers in Govind National Park practice seasonal, rotational grazing, which is generally regarded to be environmentally responsible, and often beneficial, to meadow and grassland ecosystems. Since seasonal herders only spend part of the year in any one place, the land has a chance to regenerate when they're gone, helped by the animal dung left behind, which acts as a fertilizer and seed-scatterer. In studies from around the world, this kind of grazing has been shown to keep aggressive plant species in check, allowing a wider variety of life to flourish and keeping biodiversity in balance. Despite this knowledge, it's not unusual for grazing to be forbidden in the name of conservation. Of many examples, I'll give you two.

The shallow wetlands of Rajasthan's Keoladeo National Park are the winter home to tens of thousands of birds—including critically endangered Siberian Cranes—and are a monsoon-season breeding ground for flocks of herons, storks, ibises and egrets. Local herders used to graze their buffaloes there, but once the area became a national park they were banned. With the cattle gone, grasses grew wildly, choking the marshes and seriously degrading the quality of the habitat for birds. Park authorities then had to engage in perpetual grass removal efforts—which were once handled naturally by the buffaloes. Clearly, the buffaloes had contributed greatly to the creation of an ecosystem that was perfect avian habitat.

Much closer to Govind, in the Himalayas of Uttarakhand, sits the famed Valley of Flowers National Park, once home to 520 plant species. A number of studies have shown that the eviction of the Bhotia people, who spent summers in the meadows there with their herds of sheep and goats, led to the rapid spread of knotweed, which grazing had previously kept under control. To deal with the problem, attempts were made to eradicate the knotweed by hand, which then led to an opportunistic takeover of the land by Gigantic Himalayan Balsam, the pinkish-purplish flower that carpets the valley during monsoon. While the Bhotias were there, none of these problems existed. The valley then was healthier and more botanically diverse than it is now.

By analogy, it seems quite possible that the Van Gujjars and their herds might be playing a similarly useful role in the meadows of Govind, and that their eviction could have similarly unintended environmental consequences.

Official reports on Govind, prepared by the state of Uttarakhand in 2009, say that human pressure on the park needs to be "urgently reduced" or it is "bound to suffer irreversible ecological damage." In assessing the threats described in the report, however, it's hard to distinguish how much of the impact is caused by the Van Gujjars and how much is caused by the year-round residents of the forty-two villages that abut and "fragment" the park. The loss of forested land seems mostly attributable to the villagers, who build wooden houses and granaries, cook over wood, and heat with wood throughout the frigid winter. But the report also says that the presence of livestock prevents the trees from growing back—which seems to point the finger at the nomads. At least until you do the math.

According to the report, an estimated 150,000 sheep and goats, plus another 70,000 head of "cattle, mules and horses belonging to the local inhabitants as well as migratory pastoral communities graze" in the park in the summer. Very few Van Gujjar families keep sheep and goats, so nearly all of those probably belong to the villagers. As far as the larger livestock is concerned, if there are a hundred nomadic families that use the park (as the report claims) and each family has fifty animals—which is more than Dhumman, Yusuf, or Alfa had, and would be far above average—that would total just 5,000 animals in Van Gujjar hands. And that's surely an overestimate. So, either about 65,000 cattle, mules and horses—plus virtually all of the sheep and goats—belong to the families of forty-two mountain villages, who would be responsible for the vast majority of any environmental damage due to grazing—or the figures in the report are less than accurate. And if the figures are off, it's more difficult to trust the conclusions that are based on them. (From what I knew about the veracity of some of the reports written about Rajaji, in which areas were cleared of Van Gujjars on paper, but not on the ground, I had reason to question the numbers.)

I spoke with one of the authors of the Govind report—Dr. G.S. Rawat, a prominent biologist at the Wildlife Institute of India—in June 2009. He sympathized with the Van Gujjars, speaking about them as good, honest people, and acknowledging that they had nothing to do with wildlife poaching. Rawat was also the only contributor to the report who suggested compensating the nomads to settle their land rights claims, rather than just banning them from the park. Yet he had no doubts that the buffaloes were hurting the ecosystem and diminishing fragile wildlife habitat. Even more than grazing, he said, the biggest problem was that they trampled seedlings to death with their heavy hooves. And he noted that since families and herds had grown, there were more nomads bringing more livestock up to the meadows than ever before. Rawat said that their increasing numbers had made the Van Gujjars' use of Govind's *bugyals* (meadows) unsustainable; they had to go.

But I also spoke with Nabi Jha, a scientist and former research fellow at the G.B. Pant Institute of Himalayan Environment and Development who specializes in mountain grasslands ecology. He believes that seasonal rotational grazing is good for mountain meadows, and he firmly opposes the plan to evict the Van Gujjars from Govind, at least at this time. No one, he said, had ever determined the environmental impact of the nomads' herds, or how many animals the meadows in the park could sustainably support. "We need to measure the land's carrying capacity against the buffaloes' demands before we'll know if there's any reason to ban Van Gujjars or limit their numbers," he said.

Thinking logically, Rawat's point about the dangers of expanding herds can't be ignored. With ever-increasing numbers of buffaloes, one must conclude that at some point they will reach critical mass, surpassing the land's carrying capacity, both in the high meadows and in the forests of the Shivalik Hills. But, as Nabi Jha notes, no one knows whether that has happened yet or how soon that will occur. And it's possible that there are solutions yet to be considered that can protect wildlife habitat without the wholesale, unilateral eviction of the Van Gujjars, especially since they are only one of many factors impacting the ecosystems in which they live.

In fact, when I recently spoke with Rawat again, in November 2014 (over five years after our first conversation) his opinion had shifted and was more attuned with Jha's. He said that more study was necessary before any intelligent policy could be developed, for the very same reasons that Jha cited. And he stepped away from his previous assertion that the Van Gujjars should be removed from the park; instead, he suggested some kind of involvement by or assistance from the state, perhaps supplying the nomads with a certain amount of free fodder to mitigate their needs, or maybe expanding the territories on which they are allowed to graze, to dilute the intensity of their impact.

When I asked him about the number of livestock that the 2009 report estimated were grazing in Govind, he said he had no idea how accurate those figures were, since they were provided by the forest department. He agreed that if those numbers were even close to correct, then the Van Gujjars' buffaloes would be only a "small fraction" of the total, and that their removal alone would not greatly reduce the threats to the park's wildlife habitat.

Manto didn't think that defending the environment had much at all to do with why the park authorities wanted the Van Gujjars out. "These guys are full of themselves," he told me in Dehradun in 2009. "They see the parks as their own private fiefdoms and want to show them off to other officials and foreign tourists, and they don't want a bunch of poor herders around spoiling the view." It had a familiar ring to it: Who would visit Yellowstone if Shoshone hunting parties were roaming around and camping along its rivers? And what tourists to the Masai Mara wanted to see tribespeople and cows sharing the savannah with the wildlife?

Still, as I tried to grasp the truth of the situation, to understand from as impartial a perspective as possible what kind of threat the Van Gujjars actually posed to the forests and meadows of Govind National Park, it was difficult to know exactly what—or who—to believe.

On the other hand, it was viscerally clear how being banned from the park would threaten the families that called it home.

Inside Director Rasaily's office, Dhumman and the other *lambardars* didn't present the forest department honchos with philosophical or scientific arguments about the eco-sustainable traditional practices of the Van Gujjars or indigenous peoples in general. They let Manto make the case that blocking the Van Gujjars would violate the Forest Rights Act, while they themselves simply asked for mercy for their families.

When they emerged, the Van Gujjars who'd been waiting outside crowded around to hear the news. It wasn't good. Dhumman, with an expression at once pained and almost amused, as though the absurdity of the situation was nearly laughable but not quite, calmly explained the results of the meeting. Rasaily offered them nothing. The gates of Govind hadn't budged an inch. Beyond Rasaily's adherence to the Wildlife Protection Act of 1972—which should have been superseded by the Forest Rights Act—the main sticking point seemed to be the director's assertion that since the families migrating to Govind wintered in U.P., they had no right to use the resources of Uttarakhand.

It was a disappointing blow, but not entirely unexpected. Upon receiving the decision, there was no shouting, there were no angry threats, and there was no violence. The Van Gujjars simply walked away, out to the main road, and were shuttled to the RLEK office for lunch, since the SOPHIA office was much too small.

I began to follow along, but Manto told me that Director Rasaily wanted to meet me. It seemed a bit strange, but Manto said, "Just go in and say hi. It'll only take a minute. I'll wait out here, then we'll head to RLEK together." I walked towards the office, glad to have this unexpected chance to talk to the man who had pledged to keep the Van Gujjars out of Govind and who, with a word, could allow them in. Though of course I sympathized with the Van Gujjars, I had wondered if maybe Rasaily was simply a staunch advocate for the environment who truly believed that the buffalo herders would destroy precious wildlife habitat if they remained in the parks. Perhaps the disagreement over the rights of the nomads to access their meadows was an honest difference of opinion between a man who prioritized conservation over all else, and the people who would be hurt by his decisions.

Rasaily, standing behind his desk, welcomed me in, shook my hand, and offered me a seat facing his, with the desk between us. He looked at me over the top of a pair of wire-rimmed spectacles that were perched on the tip of his nose. The front half of his head was bald, while the back half was covered with short graying hair. His skin was cappuccino-colored, and he had a faint gray moustache. To the left of the desk stood a bookcase filled with titles such as *Saving Wild Lands* and *The Wildlife of India*. There were twelve other men in the room, wearing uniforms with stars on their lapels, looking dour. They sat behind and to the side of me.

There wasn't much chit-chat.

"Are you with the press?" Rasaily asked.

I said, "No."

"Are you an Indian citizen?"

"No."

"Then what are you doing here?" he asked, rhetorically and angrily, raising his voice. "I can have you arrested for being a foreigner participating in a political rally!" He smacked his hand down on his desk.

This was definitely not what I was expecting. I didn't even know how to respond, and before I could come up with anything half-intelligent to say, Rasaily pressed on against me.

"You are an outside political agitator, a foreigner making trouble in India, and there are serious consequences for that!" he said, seeming to have found a theme that he liked.

"I'm not agitating anything or anyone," I answered, finally finding my tongue. "Even if I wanted to agitate these people, how could I? I don't speak Hindi! I can't even talk to them."

My logic, which seemed self-evident, was lost on him. He continued to accuse me of meddling in local politics so, seeing no reason to endure his baseless tirade, I stood up to leave. I took a couple of steps towards the door, but three of the uniformed men leapt up, grabbed me, and physically held me back. With no choice, I sat down, furious and a bit frightened.

I wanted to lash out at Rasaily, telling him he had no right or reason to keep me against my will. I wanted to dare him to arrest me, to make an international incident out of this and draw attention not only to how he dealt with me, but how he was shutting the Van Gujjars out of their meadows, destroying families and an age-old culture. But I didn't say any of that. I opted, instead, for what I thought would be a smarter strategy—placating him and playing stupid, figuring he'd eventually see that I was no threat, get bored, and release me. I calmly tried to explain that Manto had invited me to join him at the park headquarters, and that I had no idea whatsoever that as a foreigner I shouldn't have been there (if that was even true). I apologized for the mistake, and said that it was based in ignorance, not malice. I even tried telling him that I was an environmentalist who loved national parks and agreed that nature needed to be preserved. Rasaily, however, wasn't swayed.

He demanded to see my passport, but I lied and told him I didn't have it with me; there was no way I was putting that kind of control into his hands. "How can you not have it with you?!" he shouted. "That is also a crime!" He picked up the phone, made a call, and said something in Hindi. My main worry, at this point, was that he was going to try to force me to give him the memory card from my camera or, worse, the camera itself.

Instead, he pulled out a piece of paper and handed me a pen, commanding me to "write a statement explaining what you were doing at the rally." So I wrote that I had come at Manto's invitation, that I was not engaged in any political agitation or activity, and that the whole incident was based on a big misunderstanding.

Rasaily insisted that I make a few changes to it, like specifically naming the office at which the rally had taken place as well as the NGO that Manto ran. Once I did that, he told me to add that I was participating in a political rally. I refused. He repeated his order, and I refused again.

Just then a policeman who looked no older than twenty came through the door—responding to the phone call Rasaily had made. Once Rasaily explained his version of the situation to him, the policeman enthusiastically agreed that I had done something terribly illegal and that he was arresting me on charges of being a foreign political agitator. It seemed like I had entered a story Kafka might have written if he'd lived in South Asia—but as strange and scary as the prospect of going to jail was, at least, I thought, I'd be out of Rasaily's office. By this time, I'd been in there for nearly thirty minutes.

The door opened and I was escorted into the parking lot. Manto and Namith were gone. The young policeman opened the side door of a white SUV. I didn't get in. His partner, who was standing beside the vehicle, unslung his rifle from his shoulder and trained it directly on me. It was hard to imagine that he would actually shoot me, but the way the morning had gone thus far, I decided I'd better not risk it. I got in the car.

The driver sped through the streets of Dehradun, as quickly as traffic would allow. Various scenarios ran through my mind. On one hand, it was impossible to imagine that I could possibly spend any significant amount of time behind bars, because the charges against me were so ridiculous. Still, I was deeply rattled. My biggest fear was that I'd have to abandon the migration, that the project I'd already deeply invested myself in would turn to dust.

My mouth was so dry I could hardly swallow. I'd finished all of the water I carried earlier in the morning, and the driver refused to stop for any.

When we reached police headquarters, I was marched into a room whose light blue walls were scuffed and peeling. Only a few people occupied the rows of wooden benches that faced a table at which no one was sitting. After a couple of minutes, a police officer emerged from another room.

He came over to greet me, and I breathed a sigh of relief. I could tell at once, just by his demeanor, that he was a reasonable man. He asked me my name and my nationality and requested to see my passport—which I immediately handed to him. He looked it over and gave it back, then wanted to know why I had been brought in. I told him my mouth was so parched it was hard to talk, so he brusquely ordered the young policeman who had arrested me to bring me some mineral water.

Once I'd taken a few sips, I explained what had happened and what I'd been doing at the Rajaji Park headquarters in the first place. He listened, nodding, and when I said Rasaily had had me arrested as a foreign political agitator, he rolled his eyes. I phoned Manto—who had gone to the RLEK office once he realized he wasn't going to be able to get into Rasaily's office to help me—to verify my story, and put him on the phone with the officer. When they were finished, the officer handed the phone back to me, and Manto said he would come to the police station right away. The officer looked at me with a half-smile. "I'm sure you haven't done anything wrong," he said. "I'm going to let you go."

I shook his hand and thanked him profusely. He asked if I'd like some chai, but I politely declined, saying I was supposed to meet some friends and was already quite late.

As I walked out of the building and towards the street to wait for Manto, a newspaper reporter fell in step beside me. He starting asking questions about my detention and the events leading up to it, but I didn't want to talk. My goal was to continue migrating with Dhumman's family and, after my encounter with Rasaily, it seemed wisest to keep a low profile.

Manto picked me up in his Maruti minivan, and I told him the story from beginning to end. He was deeply apologetic for encouraging me to meet Rasaily. But, he said, "At least now you see the kind of man the Van Gujjars are dealing with." He added that he had alerted one of the newspapers about my arrest after I had phoned him, thinking that if a story was published, it would be an embarrassment for Rasaily, who would be seen as having terrorized a tourist. I said I wished he hadn't done that, thinking it'd be better if everyone forgot about the whole thing, but Manto assured me I had no reason to be concerned. Later, it turned out, sympathetic stories did run in several newspapers; one bore a headline in Hindi that read "We're sorry Michael, we're so ashamed!" and offered an apology for the way a government official had treated a foreign visitor to Dehradun.

When I got out of the van at the RLEK office, Dhumman and Yusuf came over immediately to make sure I was all right. Their concern was genuine, and I was touched by it. Manto explained to them what had happened, and they listened, slowly shaking their heads. They then filled in the details for the other Van Gujjars who were lingering in the back yard, while I went inside to see if there was any food left in the kitchen.

The cars that had picked us up in the morning were just about to make their return trip, so Dhumman, Yusuf, Alfa, Namith, and the others piled in and left for Kalsi. I was famished, so I stayed behind and ate, and talked with Manto and his father, Avdhash, for a while, then took a bus back to Kalsi later in the afternoon, reaching our camp after dark. Everyone, of course, had already heard about my run-in with Rasaily, and I was greeted with chai, and questions, and the kind of laughter that expresses relief when you find out for sure that someone you care about has come through a harrowing incident unscathed.

Something subtle, but noticeable, had shifted in the way that they looked at me. Even though I certainly hadn't planned it, my friends seemed to interpret the incident in Dehradun as meaning that I was willing to go to jail for them, and they appreciated it. As the story spread among the tribe, I earned something of a reputation; after that, whenever I was introduced to Van Gujjars for the first time, most already knew who I was, and knew that I could be trusted. It also made a difference to them that I now knew first-hand who they were up against, that I had gotten a small taste of Rasaily's methods and could better understand their situation.

It made a difference to me, too. My experiences that day gave me insights into the Van Gujjars' struggles that I never would have otherwise acquired. Regardless of any legitimate arguments that might be made about the possible environmental impact of the tribe on the meadows of Govind National Park, or on the forests of Rajaji, it was crystal clear that Rasaily was not a reasonable and compassionate man who regrettably felt that he had no choice but to evict nomadic families from their traditional lands because it was the only way to save the ecosystems from certain destruction. Rather, he seemed to relish using what power he had to push around those who were weaker and more vulnerable than him. He was combative rather than conciliatory, and seemed perfectly at ease dispensing a twisted version of justice to which logic was superfluous.

That night, I felt even more like a part of the family than before. We went to sleep early, and by 2:30 AM we were awake and preparing to move.

5

THE FORK
IN THE ROAD

❧

The road out of Kalsi climbed steeply as it curled around a ridge, following the Yamuna into the gorge it hews through the burly Himalayan foothills. In the darkness, I could feel the change in the terrain even more than I could see it. As the shadowy slopes rose around us, I sensed their looming presence engulfing us on both sides the way you might instinctively know that someone is standing beside you, even if your eyes are shut.

A palpable energy coursed through the caravan. We were all a touch inebriated with the excitement of moving into the mountains, despite the uncertainties that lay ahead. Even the animals seemed in high spirits, walking with an extra bit of bounce, eager, it seemed, to leave the searing heat of the plains behind them.

We marched along the road, a thin ribbon of pitted asphalt that contoured around the curves of the canyon. After a few hours, dawn filled the space between the rocky ramparts that framed the river. At first, it felt like there was little to see—the cliffs were nearly sheer and the corridor they created was relatively narrow. As a result, what captured my attention more than the landscape was the water, pumping through the gouge it had carved, and was still carving, through the earth, surging over and around boulders, the sound of its rushing froth amplified by the walls of rock that contained it.

Had I been able to look down on where we were from above, perhaps from an airplane, I'd have seen that we had entered a zone of topographical transition between the plains to the south and the high, glaciated summits of the Garhwal Himalayas, to the north. But this transitional space didn't feel like a gradual one; from the ground, it felt shockingly abrupt.

As soon as you step foot into the hill country, you are dwarfed by terrain that is suddenly thrust skyward and hewn by the force of rivers and rain and wind into a muscular geologic labyrinth, a mess of towering ridges and deep waterways that instantly impress a sense of smallness and humility into anyone who isn't cursed with a pathological amount of hubris. In most parts of the world, these hills would easily be considered proper mountains in their own right, and are here only called "hills" because the major peaks behind them are so massive.

Sticking to the road, our caravan would follow the Yamuna upstream for at least a week, perhaps more—we weren't quite sure, and our plans were subject to change at any time. Day by day, as we penetrated further into the hills, the canyon opened up and the landscape became increasingly dramatic. The slopes on either side of the river grew higher and higher, kissing the sky and plunging down to the water. As impressive as they were, what truly blew my mind were the hamlets that were perched upon them. Far above the river, accessible only by a network of zigzag footpaths etched into the rocky cliffs, terraced fields of millet, wheat, and vegetables clung to mountainsides so steep, they looked like they might slide right off. Beside them sat houses made of earth and stone. I wondered who lived there, who farmed there: it was hardly possible to contemplate climbing those trails in order to come and go from one's home, let alone raising families and cultivating crops in apparent defiance of the laws of gravity.

Swaths of the hills were covered in the dark greens of deciduous forests, while the cascading patchwork of fields seemed stitched from pale greens and golds. But my main impression of the canyon's color scheme was a varied palette of browns, which changed in depth and richness over the course of a day, as the sunlight moved across bare earth and rock.

Despite the Van Gujjars' defeat at forest department headquarters in Dehradun, Dhumman still clung to a thread of hope that his family would ultimately be allowed into their meadows in

Govind National Park. But he'd also come up with an alternative plan to avert disaster in case they weren't.

While camped at Kalsi, Dhumman had connected with a friend, named Kasim, who had come to visit from Gandikhatta. Though he had been forced to settle, Kasim never relinquished the papers to his summer pasture, at a place called Kanasar. Since he wasn't going to go there, he invited Dhumman to use the meadow if he needed to, giving him a copy of his documents.

Dhumman still wanted to go to his own place, above a village named Gangar, since Kanasar was much further, higher, more remote, and was totally unfamiliar to him (though Yusuf had been there once before). Besides, he wasn't officially allowed to take his buffaloes there, either, which meant he'd have to risk going, then see if he could cut a deal with the local ranger to let his family stay for the season. But because Kanasar was not inside a national park, he was guardedly optimistic that they'd be able to work something out.

For the first week of travel past Kalsi, the route to their ancestral meadow at Gangar overlapped with the route to Kanasar. But at the village of Naugaon, the ways would split: Dhumman's usual route forked to the left, towards the Tons River, while the Kanasar route forked to the right, towards the mountains between the sacred Hindu pilgrimage sites of Yamunotri and Gangotri. The families needed to decide which way they were going to go by the time they reached Naugaon but they wanted to keep their options open until the last possible moment.

ABOVE: Seventeen-year-old Mariam leads her family's caravan through the foothills of the Himalayas, while carrying her two-year-old niece in a shawl. BELOW: Bashi watches the water buffaloes while camped at 10,000 feet above sea level.

ABOVE: A buffalo yearling with a broken leg is carried over a Himalayan pass to the meadow where the family will spend the summer. Everyone hopes the leg will heal, and the buffalo will be able to walk itself down to the lowlands in autumn. BELOW: Chamar milks a water buffalo. Buffalo milk is the main source of income for Van Gujjars, and is a major part of their diet.

Karim, four years old, getting his milk straight from the source.

Bashi tends to the herd at sunrise, along the Asan River.

ABOVE: Moving into the Himalayas, along the road that follows the Yamuna River.
BELOW: Sharafat dries off after a swim in the Yamuna River.

ABOVE: Appa makes chai with her little sister, Salma, on a chilly Himalayan morning. BELOW: Dhumman (far right) and Yusuf (second from left) meet with other Van Gujjars to figure out the best strategy to move into the mountains and avoid trouble with forest rangers.

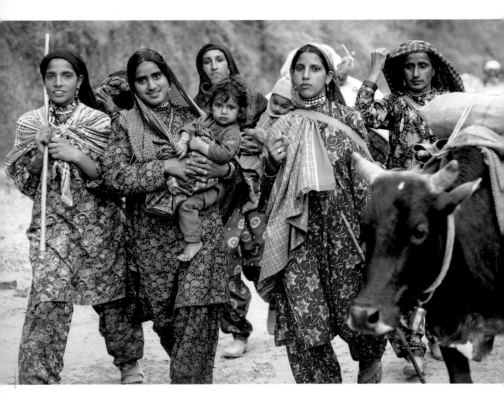

Though they are Muslim, Van Gujjar women never veil their faces—except on their wedding day.

Mariam lops leaves from a tree in the Shivalik Hills to feed the buffaloes. Van Gujjars are careful to use forest resources sustainably, knowing that they will return to the same camps year after year after year.

ABOVE: Little Halima rests on the forest floor. BELOW: A pack horse grazes among pines in the Himalayan foothills.

ABOVE: Jamila makes lunch, with some help from Yasin, while camped in the forests along the Asi Ganga River. BELOW: Mustooq, Bashi, and Salma, in the Dunda Mandal Hills.

ABOVE: Moving higher into the mountains, the family takes shelter from freezing rain under thin plastic sheets. BELOW: Van Gujjars begin milking by taking some of the buffalo's milk into their own mouths and spitting it into the mouth of the buffalo they are about to milk. They say it relaxes the animal, helping it give milk more easily.

Dhumman and his favorite buffalo.

Yusuf with his herd, along the Yamuna River.

Five-year-old Salma leads her family's caravan out the Shivalik Hills—from their secluded world behind "the veil of the forest"—on the second day of the migration.

ABOVE: The view from Kanasar, where the family ended up spending the summer.
BELOW: Buffaloes lined up along the banks of the Yamuna at Kalsi, where hundreds of migrating Van Gujjar families converge.

Hasina and her mother, Akloo. It's possible—some say likely—that Hasina's generation will be the last of the Van Gujjars to migrate to the Himalayas.

❧

Every morning, we were awake and moving long before day-break. Dhumman, Mir Hamza, and Bashi—along with Yusuf and a couple of his sons—would start off in the darkness with the buffaloes, which walk more slowly than the pack animals. Meanwhile, Jamila, Roshni, and the rest of the family would load everything on the bulls and horses, then follow. Eventually, the cargo caravan would catch up with the buffalo herd and, often, everyone would arrive together at the next camp. I usually travelled with the pack animals, since Jamila had more use for me than did Dhumman. Our goal was to get off the road as early as possible, since automobile traffic became heavier as the morning progressed. With drivers whipping around blind curves and veering recklessly when passing us, it was frighteningly obvious that vehicles were the greatest physical danger on the migration.

When we were lucky, we camped in small fields on the outskirts of the villages we travelled through. Other days, we parked ourselves on the highway's narrow shoulder, with a cliff falling away behind us and the road directly in front of us. We cooked right there. We ate right there. We slept right there. We looked like homeless refugees, with all of our belongings piled up around us, cook fires smoldering, children napping, sprawled out in the dirt at the pavement's edge. Cars and trucks sped by, unnervingly close, throwing up plumes of dust. I was sure someone was going to get killed, probably one of the little kids. But no one else seemed overly concerned. Of course, in India the margin between life and death is often measured in millimeters, so perhaps a hunk of metal and glass hurtling past with only six inches to spare is no cause for alarm, and I was just having a hard time adjusting my hyper-vigilant American sensibilities of spatiotemporal danger to local standards.

After reaching our camping spot, the routine was more or less the same each day, a variation on a theme. One crew, led by Dhumman and Yusuf, would take the buffaloes down to the river, where they'd have access to water and, ideally, could find something on which to graze. Meanwhile, another crew stayed with Jamila and Roshni to set up camp, gather firewood, haul water, cook and watch the children. A couple of people would be sent into whichever village we were staying near to sell milk and buy supplies. No one had a permanent job, and each person played a number of different roles, including me. Some days I'd help Dhumman with the herd, other days I'd stay around camp with Jamila.

When they weren't busy with chores, the young women often socialized together under Jamila's tent, since she was more easygoing than Yusuf's wife Roshni—like the "cool mom" at whose house all the neighborhood kids like to hang out. Mariam, in particular, spent quite a lot of time at our tent, as she was especially close to Appa and Goku. Khatoon and Akloo often came over, too. During the days when I stayed at camp, it wasn't unusual for me to spend a couple of hours with only women and children. Namith and I, I realized, were essentially like palace eunuchs: I was an *Angrez* with a family of my own back home, while Namith had remained single by choice and, though

Indian, was a complete foreigner to the forest world. Neither of us was a threat—nor a remotely realistic romantic option. Any protocol that might have normally guided interactions between Van Gujjar women and men from outside the family didn't apply to us. They felt perfectly at ease talking and joking around, and would sometimes get surprisingly bawdy. These hours spent with the women were some of the most relaxed and enjoyable of the entire migration, infused with an aura of pure friendship, as though we'd known each other for ages. They were happy to have us around, and shared their thoughts and feelings with surprising openness.

During one of those laid-back afternoons camped on the roadside along the Yamuna, Jamila told me that she and Dhumman were never supposed to be married. When they met, she was nineteen or twenty and betrothed to someone else. Dhumman was in his early twenties and had been married, but his wife had died. According to Jamila, she and Dhumman fell for each other instantly. Knowing that she would never be voluntarily released from her engagement, Dhumman secretly pursued her, then convinced her to run off with him and elope before her scheduled wedding day. When they returned to their families as a married couple, they had to sort out the mess of the broken arrangement, but it seemed a small price to pay to spend the rest of their lives together. They were a true love match.

Listening to the women, I learned that most of the family's marriages were in some form of upheaval—not only Appa's. Akloo had only recently returned to her husband, Gamee, and to Yusuf and Roshni's family, after spending nearly a year back with her own family. Gamee was a nice guy who I came to like a lot, but theirs was not a love match. She was in her mid-twenties and he was ten or twelve years older. He'd been married before, but his first wife and their children had died—I didn't ask how. Sometime after that, his marriage to Akloo was arranged.

Her biggest complaint was a common one among Van Gujjar women—indeed, among women everywhere: she said her mother-in-law had been unbearable to live with. Akloo felt like the servant of a short-tempered employer who demanded unrealistic levels of perfection. Roshni was impossible to please, she said, and was constantly berating her. As she told me her story, I imagined Akloo as a forest-dwelling Cinderella with no fairy godmother. She said she'd seriously considered divorce, but couldn't risk the possibility of losing her two kids in the process. Instead, she brought the situation to the *lambardars* for mediation.

After reviewing her case, the *lambardars* decided that Akloo should return to Gamee, but that they should move out from under Yusuf and Roshni's roof and into their own hut—if only a few yards away—where they could live and raise their children with more independence. They also ruled that Roshni had to treat Akloo with more respect, and that she'd have to pay a fine of 50,000 rupees to Akloo's family of origin if any kind of abuse persisted. I was impressed that an all-male council would support a young wife's rights with such clarity.

Things had improved since then, Akloo said, though it was clear that her relationship with Roshni was a bit frosty—which was another reason why she liked to spend time at Jamila's tent.

When I asked Sharafat if he knew when he would get married, he said he was engaged, but no wedding date had been set. He'd met his fiancée and she had seemed nice and was pretty enough; but she was from one of the families that had been settled in a village, so he wasn't sure how well she'd adjust to life in the forest. He was neither excited about nor resistant to the arrangements; getting married seemed like something that would just happen to him one day, like growing a beard.

As easy I usually found it to accept Van Gujjar ways on their own terms, their marriage system was the one aspect of their culture that confused me, simply because it was the one thing that didn't seem to work very well. I understood the rationale behind arranging marriages, and setting up boy-girl exchanges between families, since no parent wanted any of their children to be left without a spouse. But with all of the problems that these marriages seemed to have—which snowballed into larger problems, as the separation of one couple led to the separations of other couples—I couldn't help wondering if there might be a better way. But I couldn't think of one.

If they relied on unions rooted in romance, too many people could be left on the sidelines, with no spouse—and love marriages don't always lead to "happily ever after," anyway; between thirty and forty percent of marriages in the United States end in divorce. If, to consider the opposite solution, divorce was forbidden, that would only make couples more miserable, as there would be no way out, no hope for anything better. Maybe the problems weren't with the Van Gujjars' marriage practices as much as with the nature of long-term relationships between men and women, regardless of the cultural systems they exist within: a certain number of them are simply not going to work. The big difference between the nuptial world of the Van Gujjars and that of my own country is that it's virtually impossible for Van Gujjars to live independently without a spouse, raising the pressure to be married to existential heights.

For people for whom marriage is such a fundamental part of life, they were remarkably accepting when I told them that my girlfriend and I lived together like husband and wife, and had a child together, but had never actually wed. I didn't feel for a moment like they judged us negatively, or even like it struck them as being all that strange. They were far more surprised when I told them that we lived well over a thousand miles away from our parents, brothers or sisters; they couldn't conceive of living so far from family, or understand why anyone would choose to do so.

❧

Each day's trek along the Yamuna brought us closer to Naugaon—the fork in the road where an epic choice had to be made, which, for all of the complicated factors involved in the decision, boiled down to: left or right. A tangible aura of suspense enveloped the family, growing more and more intense as we moved up the canyon. It felt like a time bomb was tick-tick-ticking in the background, and none of us knew whether it would be diffused or explode.

Even worse than the possibility that they might have to spend the summer somewhere other than their traditional meadow was what that possibility implied: if they were banned from the park this year, they would probably be banned the next year, and the next. And once they were pushed out of their ancestral pastures, who was to say that they wouldn't get pushed out of the forests of Uttarakhand altogether? The pillars that supported their world were shaking and seemed in danger of crumbling, bringing their future crashing down around them.

Dhumman tried to get daily updates on negotiations with the forest department, regularly calling other Van Gujjars and the SOPHIA office on his cellphone to see if anyone had any news. He was visibly distracted, keeping one eye on events in Dehradun and the other on the progress of his friend Firoz, whose family was also heading to Govind National Park and was nearly a week further ahead on the road. Firoz's family would be the first to reach the gates of the park and truly test the forest department's resolve to keep them out.

Five days after we had left Kalsi and two days before we would hit Naugaon, as we camped near the village of Chmui, the signals were mixed. We knew that the chief minister of Uttarakhand had visited the town of Mori, not far from Govind National Park, and had met with Firoz and some other Van Gujjars who were already nearing the park boundary; at the meeting, local villagers voiced their support for the nomads, saying that they'd been coming to the area longer than anyone could remember, never caused trouble, and should be allowed to go to their meadows. It seemed like the chief minister had listened, but he'd made no promises.

From Dehradun, SOPHIA had alerted the national tribal welfare department, which wrote a letter to the forest department insisting that it respect the Forest Rights Act. Director Rasaily not only refused, but took out advertisements in newspapers saying that he would never allow the Van Gujjars into Uttarakhand's parks. The advertisement depicted the tribe as outsiders who were coming in to threaten the state's resources, and seemed to portray the forest department as the victim of the Van Gujjars. The people of Uttarakhand, however, as well as journalists, remained generally sympathetic to the plight of the nomads.

We stopped about a half-mile past Chmui, a small village perched on the side of the valley, with a handful of shops lining the road. Our camp was just off the pavement, on a lumpy patch of land, which was barely big enough for our two tents and all of the animals—but was much better than being stuck on the shoulder of the highway. Behind us rose a slope of loose rock, covered with trees and giant cacti; in front of us, on the other side of the road, a hotel/restaurant that was under construction sat atop a series of terraced fields that staggered steeply down to the river, about a hundred yards below.

The migration seemed like it was beginning to take a toll on the family. Goku was walking around wearing only her left shoe, since an infection on her right foot had begun to swell and abscess; it hurt her more when hard plastic rubbed against the wound than it did to walk barefoot on asphalt. Mariam struggled with a fever and a deep chest cough. Roshni was in quite a bit of pain from her arthritis, and most of the kids had green goo smeared around their nostrils. The tiny infant, Halima, who had been taken to the holy man to be cured when we were at the Asan River, was still sick.

Halima's mother, Fatima, asked me for some medication to stop her baby's fever. She knew that I'd given Roshni and Mariam Paracetamol or ibuprofen, so she was surprised when I said no. "I don't have anything for babies," I said. "All my medicine is for adults. It could kill her." Without missing a beat, she then asked if I'd give her some medicine for herself instead. "No way," I said, but I'm sure my facial expression said, "Do you think I'm stupid?" She laughed sheepishly and gave up. I don't blame her for trying—I think she didn't understand how dangerous it could have been to give Halima the medicine, and that there was no way to cut the dose for an infant.

There was no rest for the sick. Everyone had to work, regardless of how poorly they felt. I helped Mariam bring the horses and bullocks to drink at the nearest water pump, which was in the village of Chmui and had a cement trough. It was rather inconvenient to lead a few animals that far, I thought, and I wasn't looking forward to our next job: returning to the pump with the empty water jugs, then carrying them back to camp full. But as we neared our tents and were steering the pack animals off the highway, I noticed something at the building site directly across the road: a hose.

I walked over, and in the unfinished hotel dining room, which would one day have glass in the windows that looked out over the dramatic river canyon, I found the supervisor. Luckily, he spoke English. I introduced myself and made some small talk, inquiring about his building project, and he was happy to chat. After getting a quick tour of the place, I asked if the Van Gujjars I was camped with across the road could come and use his hose, since the water pump was a long way away. He smiled and said, "Why not? You are welcome," and showed me where the valve was.

I explained to Jamila that the people across the road invited us to use their hose. She seemed skeptical, but gave one jug to me and another to Goku. The four-man work crew was friendly and didn't seem to mind at all when we took some water. But later, when we needed more, no one from the family would go over without me. They didn't think the supervisor would be so welcoming if I wasn't with them.

I thought it was unnecessary, but went over with Jamila, Sharafat, and Khatoon anyway. Jamila was so uncomfortable, felt so much like she had stepped over an invisible line and into a place where she didn't belong, that as soon as one jug was full she took it and rushed quickly back to camp. Sharafat and Khatoon were more at ease, waiting patiently while the rest of the containers were filled, when we all left together. I thanked the supervisor and he shook my hand and said it had been no trouble.

Back at camp, Jamila explained that if someone from her family had asked to use the hose, the supervisor would have said no. She was sure that my white skin—dirty as it was—had won us a privilege that they would never have received on their own.

My automatic reaction was to wonder if she might have been mistaken, if she had misjudged the supervisor. After all, he seemed like a nice person, and he hadn't hesitated to extend a hospitable hand. But I also trusted Jamila. She intuitively understood the social contours, the relational topography, of her world, which was filled with subtleties and subtexts of which I was hardly aware. She was certain that, being *Angrez*, I was included in the category of people for whom it was perfectly appropriate to ask for and receive such a favor—while Van Gujjars were most definitely not.

Assuming she was right, I reasoned, if my white skin could somehow make this trip a little easier for them even in some small way, I didn't mind using it to their advantage. So far, it obviously hadn't helped at all with the only thing that really mattered: the permission.

After spending the day down by the river, Dhumman, Yusuf, and the herding crew brought the buffaloes into camp late in the afternoon. Mustooq and Mir Hamza scurried around the area where the buffaloes would eat and sleep, clearing stones from the ground so the herd would have a comfortable place to lie down. One of the calves, which spent the day separated from the adult buffaloes, slipped past Bashi, who was watching them. It ran over to its mother and starting suckling. After letting it drink for a minute, a squad of young kids was sent to steer the youngster back to its place with its age-mates. With all of her five-year-old strength, Salma whacked the calf with a *lathi*. With his inaccurate six-year-old aim, Rustem threw small rocks at it. With his two-year-old weight, Yasin grabbed its tail and pulled back. That seemed like a good idea, and soon all three kids were trying to physically drag the calf away from its mother's udders, with no success. Rustem then picked up the *lathi* and gave it a smack, without effect. As nothing seemed to be working, the children swarmed the young buffalo, pulling and prodding, shouting to each other and practically falling over themselves in their ridiculous efforts to move it. It was like a live slapstick comedy show, and their older brothers and sisters laughed at their performance until Mir Hamza eventually stepped in and easily chased the calf off.

I was watching all of this while I guarded a pile of grass, keeping the bullocks from eating the buffaloes' dinner. In one hand I held a *lathi*, in the other I cradled Hasina, the eighteen-month-old daughter of Akloo and Gamee. I swayed back and forth, singing quietly to her. I liked her a lot—she had a sweet little personality and an adorable round face with huge round eyes. She was content in my arms, listening to my song. Mustooq came over and stood beside me. He asked if I missed my own son, who was about a year older than Hasina. I told him I did, a lot. He said he missed his two kids too. Normally they would have been with us, and his wife, too—but they'd stayed back to take care of his father. Mustooq said he couldn't wait until he could return to them, though he wasn't looking forward to spending summer in the Shivaliks.

Brushing aside our moment of emotional tenderness, Mustooq changed the subject, challenging me to lift the bundle of grasses that I'd been guarding. It was still tied up as one giant bale, the way it had been carried from the fodder dealer down the road. I poked at it with my *lathi*. I tugged on the rope that bound it. "Okay," I said, and got in position, putting my back to the pile as other members of the family crowded around to watch. Most, I could tell, were already stifling their laughter. Mustooq put a cloth on top of my head to cushion the bite of the rope. The goal was to shift from a crouching position to a stand, lifting the grass off the ground and onto my back.

The smiles momentarily left the faces of my friends as anticipation took over. Might I actually lift it? They looked on as though I was about to attempt a task equal to a young King Arthur pulling Excalibur from the stone, or Arjuna shooting an arrow through the eye of the golden fish. None believed I could do it, but maybe, just maybe . . . A hush of suspense fell over them as Mustooq stepped away once the bale was properly positioned. I took a breath and strained against the rope. It was heavier than I'd expected, so I recalibrated my resolve and focused every muscle in my body on my effort to stand. I had faith in my strength, especially after the couple of weeks I'd just spent on the trail. My thighs tightened like torqued steel cables, my calves felt like compressed springs ready to pop. But try as I might, I simply couldn't straighten my legs. I wasn't even able to raise the bale an inch off the ground. At last, I pushed the rope off my head, and shrugged in defeat. Everyone burst out laughing, including me.

Thus, life went on despite the anxieties swirling powerfully beneath the surface of every moment. We worked. We played. Though everyone felt the pressure of the decision that would soon have to be made, it weighed most obviously on Dhumman, who was often so consumed in thought that it looked like a mouse might have crawled into his ear and was gnawing away at his brain. He hoped, hour by hour, for news that the forest department had finally relented and would allow his family to proceed without worry to their traditional meadow. But he knew there wasn't much time left before we would reach Naugaon, and he struggled with what we should do once we got there if nothing had changed by then.

The next morning, as always, we loaded up and headed out before daybreak. A few other families also happened to be on the move, and for about an hour, as night faded into the vague luminescence that is dawn at the bottom of a canyon, multiple herds merged together, turning the road into a living river of buffalo horns and hides and hooves. When we pulled out of the flow just past the village of Bornigad, we were joined by Dhumman's cousin, Alfa, and his family. From here on, I learned, they would travel with us for the rest of the migration, regardless of which way we turned at Naugaon. And, I was told, that choice would have to be made in a matter of hours, as our next camp, along either route, would lie beyond the fork in the road.

Making ourselves as much at home as possible on the side of the road, where the uneven edge of the asphalt was overtaken by a rim of packed dirt, Goku and Salma swept away the top layer of loose dust with whisks made of twigs. Jamila and Sharafat stacked the saddlebags, and Appa sparked the cook fire. Meanwhile, Mustooq, Mir Hamza and Bashi—along with crews from Yusuf's and Alfa's families—led the buffaloes down the hillside behind us to the river, which was still shrouded in shadow, waiting to be touched by the sunlight that was slowly spreading down the cliff behind it. There, by the water's edge, the animals would be comfortable, and would be safely tucked away from the vehicles that sped dangerously past our camp.

After Appa served up the morning tea, Dhumman and Alfa flagged down a shared jeep that was heading north to the town of Purola, where there was a forest department ranger station that could give them a first-hand update on the permit situation, and where they could meet with their friend Firoz and get his input.

Everyone else waited for them to come back with the information, or at least with better-informed guesses, that would surely sway their fate. While a few people—including Jamila, Roshni, and Alfa's wife Sakina—stayed on the roadside, enduring the heat and dust to keep an eye on the camp, most of us went down to the river. A bridge overhead cast a substantial swath of shade on the bank of smooth, rounded rocks. The translucent green water flowed clear and cold and deep. The guys stripped down to their skivvies and plunged right in. We swam out to a rock in the middle of the river, which we climbed up on and leaped off of, splashing back into the current. When they were ready to dry off, they found big buffaloes that were lying in the sun and sprawled out on their backs, using them as horned, hairy lounge chairs. The young women also wanted to bathe and get cool, so they walked around a bend in the river, out of sight.

By the time Dhumman and Alfa returned, the sunlight had begun to climb the valley walls, leaving the river and our camp in shadows once again. A thin haze hung in the air like gold dust. The heat of the day had inched its way into retreat. Jamila, Roshni, and a few of the older children sat in a circle on the side of the road with Dhumman and Alfa to hear what they had to report. The news was discouraging. The forest rangers, they said, had told them that nothing had changed, and they were under orders not to allow Van Gujjars into meadows of Govind. Their conversation with Firoz confirmed it: his family had been stopped at the forest gates near the village of Naitwar and was blocked from entering the national park. They were camped on the road, waiting, in a place where there was little fodder available to scrounge or to purchase. If they headed up to their meadow, they could reap unlimited fines or face arrest and have their herd confiscated. So they stayed where they were, stuck in limbo, hoping they could enter the forest before they ran out of food for their buffaloes.

Dhumman spelled out the dilemma. On one hand, if he and Yusuf and Alfa stuck to their usual route and joined Firoz, their combined presence might be enough to pressure the forest department to let them all into the park. But if it wasn't, if Raisaily or his superiors in the government still wouldn't budge, the combined presence of all their families would deplete the scant resources in the area four times faster, hastening the arrival of disaster for them all.

On the other hand, Kanasar would be a more difficult place to spend the summer than their meadows at Gangar, and going there would be perceived as a victory for the forest department, which could set a dire precedent for the future. But standing up for themselves and losing would be even worse. Neither choice was a good one.

As they weighed the options and their consequences, visions of hundreds of buffaloes starving on the roadside with nowhere to go ultimately swayed their minds. They simply couldn't risk going to Gangar; they could lose everything. So, they would turn right at Naugaon and aim for Kanasar, where, despite the hardships involved in reaching the meadows there, they felt more confident that they'd ultimately be able to get their buffaloes to grass. It seemed like probably the better of two bad possibilities, but their decision was riddled with doubts.

With their plan set, Dhumman and Alfa went into Bornigad to inquire about hiring a cargo truck to carry all the buffalo calves and the young children to their next camp, which was up an unusually long, steep section of road. Knowing that soon they'd have some unavoidably strenuous days, the adults didn't want their little ones—human or bovine—to overdo it now, especially with some of the children already sick.

The truck came at about 2 AM. The small children, twelve of them, were hoisted up into the cab. They waited there quietly with Roshni and Fatima while everyone else gathered at the back of the vehicle, forming a human corral around the calves. There was no ramp, so the young buffaloes had to be lifted up, pushed from behind and pulled from the front in order to get them into the cargo bed, and the animals were not thrilled at this idea. They struggled and flailed and had be to muscled in by as many people as could get a hand on them, who tried to be as forceful as they needed to be yet as gentle as possible. I felt like I was watching a weird rodeo event, lit entirely by a few weak flashlights.

Once the calves were in, the saddlebags were slung over the beams that ran across the top of the cargo bed, which would make the trek much less strenuous on the horses and bulls. As long as we were making things easy, I loaded my big backpack into the truck, too, keeping only a small bag with some camera gear and a water bottle with me. As soon as Jamila and Sakina squeezed into the jam-packed cab and managed to close the cab door behind them, the truck groaned up the road toward Barkot.

Those of us who stayed with the adult buffaloes and pack animals set off on foot, knowing, for the first time on the migration, where we were ultimately heading, and knowing that it wasn't the familiar *bugyal* that my companions thought of as home. The mood on the road was different than on any previous morning, as though something profound was taking place. Even though I could hardly see anyone else in the darkness, I could feel it. And I could hear it. On most days, one or two people might sing quietly to themselves, for a few minutes here or a few minutes there, while they walked. But on this day, as they moved through the darkness, my friends all sang together, with more passion, more volume, and for a greater distance than ever before.

6

NOT THE LIFE
OF A FOOL

🌰

W e found the women and children on the side of the road, a mile or so before the town of Barkot. The three families had set up camp beside one another in what felt like a particularly precarious spot, along a narrow strip of dirt where there was virtually no space between the tire tracks imprinted on the ground and the sheer slope that fell towards the Yamuna far below. My friends clearly placed great faith in the goodwill and technical skill of Garhwali drivers—or in their god.

On our long uphill trek from Bornigad, we'd climbed through the darkness into a new climate zone. Here, the hills were covered by pines that cast long, slender shadows through the golden glow of daybreak, which gradually filled the spaces between the trees like a tide of light rising from the east. The morning air smelled fresh and clean and felt invigorating.

After some chapatis and chai, I walked into Barkot with Sharafat, Hamju, and Alfa's son Kalu, who carried the families' fresh milk to sell at a dairy shop. An important transportation hub, the town's main market was bustling with people getting on and off buses and claiming seats in shared jeeps, which might carry them towards Yamunotri, or the Tons Valley, or Mussoorie, or Uttarkashi. I split from my companions, searching the busy bazaar for someplace with a computer and an internet connection, then picking up a few items that Jamila had requested: sugar, rice, atta, and vegetables. Before heading back to camp, I stopped into a pharmacy to purchase some antibiotics for Goku, whose foot infection was getting worse every day. If it didn't get treated before we went up into the mountains, I feared it could become a serious problem for her.

Back at camp, I took out the tourist map of Uttarakhand that was buried in my backpack. Now that our course was set, I wanted to see where we were going and how we would get there. Kanasar, however, wasn't labelled on the map and, since my friends couldn't read, no one could even point out its general location; to them, the map might as well have been a piece of abstract art. By asking about places that were near Kanasar, however, and finding them on the map, I was able to get a rudimentary idea of where it was—east of the village of Hanuman Chatti, which was on the way to Yamunotri, and west of a small but well-known lake called Dodi Tal.

It was clear that the most direct way to get to Kanasar would be to continue following the Yamuna to Hanuman Chatti, then swing east and climb into the mountains. But, I learned, we weren't going to go that way. Instead, we would take a roundabout route, making a deliberate long-cut that would add a substantial number of miles to our journey but which, all things considered, was the best approach to the alpine meadow.

Since Kanasar was about 3300 feet higher than their traditional *bugyal* near Gangar, we had to pace our ascent to make sure we didn't get there before the snow had had a chance to melt and the grass had come up. The problem with simply lingering down along the Yamuna was the *yatra*—or pilgrimage—season, which was just getting underway. Over the next few weeks, thousands of Hindu pilgrims would travel to and from the temple at Yamunotri, near the source of the river. They would come and go in buses, cars and vans, hurtling recklessly along the narrow, rough road that snakes up the canyon. My companions feared that the surge of *yatra* traffic that would soon be flooding the road would pose a real danger to life, limb, and livestock. Additionally, the whole area would be overpopulated, and Dhumman knew that they'd have to pay exorbitant prices to locals for places to camp and keep their herds, and he doubted whether there would be enough fodder to support them for long.

Hence, we would leave the Yamuna Valley, cutting up and over a bastion of steep, forested hills, then dropping down into the Bhagirathi River valley. There, we might have to contend with some early *yatra* traffic to Gangotri—near the source of the sacred Ganges River—but only for a day or two, since we'd quickly turn onto a quiet side road, along a small tributary, which would lead to open forest where fodder was plentiful and free. Once we got there, we could meander comfortably, at our own pace, before making the final push to Kanasar.

❦

We passed though Barkot before dawn, while the town was still asleep. Hiking well into the morning, we eventually left the road and camped along a creek in a small clearing at the cusp of the woods, just off a footpath that led into the Dunda Mandal Hills.

Though no one was happy about abandoning Gangar for the summer, the simple fact that we now knew where we were going had lifted some of the tension from the caravan. And everyone was relieved to get off the road for a few days. Dhumman, in particular, seemed much more relaxed and less distracted, with time for casual conversation and laughter. That afternoon, I told him what Jamila told me about how the two of them had met and married, and he waved a hand in protest. "No, no, no, it didn't happen like that," he said. "I didn't talk her into any-thing! *She* seduced me and convinced *me* to run away with *her*, even though she was engaged." Jamila jumped in to disagree, and the two of them bickered good-naturedly, like any married couple with different versions of the same story, neither able to believe that the other couldn't remember how one of the most important events in their lives had actually transpired. It would have been impossible to talk to Dhumman like this a day or two earlier, when his head was so wrapped up in the dilemma he faced, and I was glad that he had at last returned to himself.

Like most people in confusing circumstances, my friends were awash in emotional contradictions. Dhumman was more at ease, but now had a set of new concerns about taking his family somewhere that was totally unfamiliar to him. Likewise, Sharafat was excited about having a chance to see new places, but was nervous about heading into the unknown. Appa was truly sad that they weren't going to Gangar—she longed to return to the home she'd missed over the two summers that she'd spent in her husband's village—but she was curious about what they'd find at Kanasar. Jamila was resigned to their fate, and worried about it, and angry about it, too.

From our camp at the foot of the Dunda Mandal Hills, Dhumman spoke to Manto on the phone. It looked as though the chief wildlife warden of Uttarakhand—Raisaily's boss—was going to sign an order allowing the Van Gujjars into Govind National Park very soon. But in the meantime, Firoz, who was still waiting on the roadside outside the park, had exhausted all the local sources of fodder; SOPHIA was going to send them a truckload of grass, which Manto hoped would last until the buffaloes were allowed into the park. If the situation became truly dire, Firoz was prepared to sneak into forest with his herd. And if he was sent to jail for it, he said defiantly, at least he wouldn't have to worry about where his next meal was coming from.

For a moment, the families reconsidered their plan. If they would be permitted to enter the park after all, perhaps they should turn around and head in that direction. But after a quick conference among Dhumman, Yusuf, and Alfa, they decided not to. I didn't quite understand their reasoning. Even if Firoz was suffering from a fodder shortage now, it would take my companions at least a week to reach the forest gate at Govind, and it sounded like by that time they'd probably be allowed straight up to their meadows. The problem, Dhumman explained, was that "probably" was only a half-promise at best. They couldn't afford to reverse course based on "probably"—they required more certainty than that. Until the chief wildlife warden actually put pen to paper, they couldn't trust that he would. They had too much to lose. That made a certain amount of sense to me, but there was something about how quickly they rejected the idea of turning around that made me wonder if they simply had an aversion to retracing their steps, if maybe there was an entrenched taboo among Van Gujjars that forbade backtracking on migration.

Our course confirmed, we moved deeper into the Dunda Mandal Hills, and for the first few days, everyone was grateful to be back in the forest. We camped on earth rather than asphalt, in peaceful groves of pine. The animals could wander and graze freely, with no worries about them devouring a farmer's crops or being struck by a speeding car. We were again out of sight, behind the veil, where my friends felt most comfortable. This was their element.

But not exactly. Unlike their territory in the Shivaliks and at Gangar, where they are as familiar with the topography and the ecology as most people are with their bedrooms, here they were strangers. More than once, forks in the trail created moments of bewilderment and debate over which way to go. The buffaloes were even more perplexed. They knew the way to Gangar by heart and never had to be directed or steered; they led the way there, and the people followed. In this new place, and for the rest of the migration, the buffaloes strayed from the path, paused randomly, and had to be led and prodded forward, dawdling with no sense of purpose.

The trek to the high ridge that divided the Yamuna and Bhagirathi Valleys was unexpectedly strenuous—much longer and steeper than hiking out of the Shivaliks had been, and far more difficult than their usual route to Gangar. Some of the kids who'd had no problems hiking along the road were pressed to their limits, but there weren't enough free arms or backs on which to carry them all. Djennam Khatoon, the three-and-a-half-year-old daughter of Chamar and Fatima, walked barefoot up the trail, weeping with every step. Her older brother, Rustem, aged six, wore mismatched plastic shoes and an expression of misery on his dirt-smeared little face. Jamila asked me to help with them, so I did what I could. Since I was already hauling a huge backpack, the best I could do was to offer them each a hand. Djennam Khatoon gripped my left pinky and immediately stopped crying. Rustem curled his little fingers around my right ring and middle fingers, and seemed to take some strength from them. As I did when my own son was upset, I sang quietly to them, which was just enough of a distraction to ease their pain. We walked onward and upward together.

I couldn't imagine an American family doing this with their children. We hesitate to take our little kids on long road trips out of concern that it would be too difficult for them to spend hour after hour in the car; forget about marching them into the Himalayas without shoes. It's not that my companions were cruel or unconcerned about their children; they kept a keen eye on how the kids were doing, and didn't want to push them too far past their limits—but they were okay with nudging them right up to that line. They knew that their children had to grow up to be tough, prepared to handle a life of unending physical demands, and there was no point in creating any kind of illusions that their world was a soft or easy place.

As we gained elevation, the trail snaked steeply over ribs of rock, upwards through the woods. The light became gauzy, hanging between the trees like a translucent amber curtain, given density by smoke wafting from forest fires burning on nearby slopes. We made camp just below the pass, near where Dhumman and Yusuf believed we'd find a spring. After a futile search, they realized they had been mistaken or misinformed, the victims of their own ignorance of the terrain.

We had no choice but to send a team to fetch water from the last source we'd passed—a small stream about a mile back down the steepest part of the trail. I went with them, and it was all good fun, letting gravity whisk us downhill, then playing and joking around by the creek—until it came time to haul the full jugs back up. We were more exhausted from the morning's climb than we'd realized, and the weight of the water made for a grueling ascent. When we finally reached the high camp, Goku put down her load and burst into tears.

Though she was only fourteen, she was as strong as any young Olympic athlete—but she also had a seriously infected foot, and walking on it was torturing her. This day, the pain had broken her. I looked at her wound and expressed puzzlement at the fact that it had continued to get worse, when she confessed that she hadn't been taking the antibiotics I'd bought for her. She was intimidated by the size of the pills. This was the first time I got angry on the migration. She *had* to take the medicine, I insisted, or it was possible the infection could cost her her foot—the abscess looked that bad. If the pills were too big we could cut them into smaller pieces, or crush them and put them into her food, I said, but she *had* to take them. Jamila was visibly surprised by the intensity of my reaction, and agreed to make sure Goku took the pills.

As twilight began to settle over the hills, we spotted a forest fire burning further down the ridge. We could see the flames devouring entire trees, and the loud cracking and popping of igniting timbers sounded like the noise in a large city during Diwali. An acrid haze shrouded our camp. Though the blaze covered a fairly small area, it seemed to be hungry and was spreading aggressively. Since I'm from the American West, where each year we have massive wildfires that can consume tens of thousands of acres in a day, I wondered if we were too close. I asked Jamila what she thought, and she said she was keeping an eye on it, paying attention to wind speed and direction, but she didn't think we were in any imminent danger. She was more concerned that the forest department would blame us for sparking the fire.

As we continued talking, Jamila confessed to some serious reservations about their entire plan. While she agreed that they could not have gone to Gangar this summer, she wished they'd found a different alternative. Kanasar, she thought, was simply too far, too high, too cold, and too remote, especially with so many small children in their caravan. Since the family that traditionally used it hadn't been there in a number of years, she knew they'd have to rebuild their old hut, or perhaps construct a new one from scratch. And they weren't even sure if the forest rangers would let them in. She thought that Yusuf may have persuaded Dhumman that Kanasar was a good option because he believed that milk prices would be higher near there than in some of the other places they might have tried to go. But she didn't think a few extra rupees would be worth the risks and difficulties they'd surely encounter.

Weighing on her mind as much or more than these logistical concerns was the outlook for the future. Having abandoned Gangar this year, what would happen next year? Would they be allowed back in then? If not, would they try Kanasar again, or somewhere else? And would the forest department attempt to keep them out of Uttarakhand altogether? The prospects were unnerving. The age-old rhythms and patterns of her tribe's way of life had been disrupted, and Jamila didn't know what, if anything, they'd be able to rely on in the years to come. The only thing that gave her some sense of comfort was the knowledge that it would all unfold according to Allah's will.

Perhaps that was why, with so much on her mind, she was able to keep her cool and her sense of humor intact. Or perhaps that was just her innate personality. Despite the very real concerns she had about the immediate and distant future, she remained patient and fully present, easy to talk to and laugh with.

As Jamila held Yasin on her lap, she went on to say that she knew that many mainstream Indians looked down on Van Gujjars for their nomadic lifestyle, but she was proud of it and didn't want to give it up. "Many people think that we are fools for not settling in villages," she said. "But look at what we have! We go with the weather, so now we're heading where the air is cool, where you can get a good night's sleep, when down below it is too hot. We go where there is plenty of water, while down below people will be fighting for it. In the summer, we don't have to deal with mosquitoes or malaria or scorpions or snakes or many other problems. We think that what's good for our buffaloes is also good for us. Does this sound like the life of a fool?"

It did not.

⁂

With no cars to worry about, we slept later than usual, leaving camp all together as the darkness washed from the sky, the pale violet dawn mixing with the smoke still rising from the ridge to the south. Within minutes we were over the pass atop the Dunda Mandal Hills and descending from the divide, switchback after dusty switchback. With each step, my quadriceps felt like they were being pounded into pulp, as they fought the force of gravity that wanted to pull me and my pack straight down the mountainside. Still, it was much easier than walking up the other side had been.

After two more days, we emerged along the two-lane highway that ran alongside the Bhagirathi River. Downstream, to the south, the river would merge with the Alaknanda to become the Ganga. All the way upstream, the waters flowed out of the glacier at Gaumukh, above the temple at Gangotri where Lord Shiva is said to have caught the sacred river in his nest of matted hair, cushioning its impact as it fell from the heavens so it didn't destroy the earth—though sometimes, during monsoon season, it seems like it might yet.

We turned north, upriver, towards the town of Uttarkashi. The quiet of the hills was quickly dashed by cargo trucks, whose drivers didn't hesitate to express their frustrations when herds of buffaloes slowed them down. Honking horns and belching exhaust, they passed with engines roaring. We travelled on for a mile or two before stopping on a thin lip of the road shaded by a few pine trees. The animals could graze in a patchwork of fields stitched together on the narrow floodplain some fifty yards below our camp.

Along the way, we'd passed another Van Gujjar family, and Dhumman had taken a few minutes to stop and chat with his friend, Noor Ahmed, who possessed more current information about the situation with the forest department. He reported that migrating families were being screened at every forest entry checkpoint in Uttarakhand. Nomads who had been given land in the Rajaji Park compensation deals were being blocked from their ancestral meadows, since they had signed away their rights to access the forests with their herds. Of course, neither Dhumman, Yusuf, nor Alfa had received any land—but Kasim, whose grazing documents they planned to use to gain entry to Kanasar, did.

If Noor Ahmed was right, the rangers would have a list of the Van Gujjars who had settled in Gandikhatta, Kasim's name would surely appear on it, and my friends and their buffaloes would be turned away when they tried to enter the forest. The very papers that had seemed like their salvation could prove to be their downfall.

The anxieties that had temporarily dissipated in the hills seethed once more. The forest gate we had to pass through was not far beyond Uttarkashi, at a village called Gangori (not to be confused with Gangar, or Gangotri). If we were stopped there, it would pose an insurmountable problem, since we were already on Plan B and Dhumman had no Plan C. At this point, there was nowhere else to go. "I think we're doomed," Dhumman said, despondently, as concern clouded his face. But we couldn't stop where we were, and it was too late for the families to turn around and try for their own meadows in Govind National Park. There was nothing to do but press ahead and hope that the forest rangers manning the gates could be reasoned with.

7

THE FOREST GATE

🌿

W e reached the outskirts of Uttarkashi the next
morning, stopping at a terraced plot of land just
off the highway where a dozen other Van Gujjar
families were already camped. Most of the caravans whose summer
meadows lay beyond Uttarkashi halted here first, waiting until
after midnight to walk their herds through the major market town.
Along the length of the terraces, tents were pitched side-by-side,
creating the feeling of an improvised bazaar, but with nothing for
sale. The buffaloes were led across the road and down a hill to the
farmland that blanketed the banks of the Bhagirathi.

This would be our last stop before the forest barrier at Gangori. If we were going to be shut out of the mountains for using the paperwork of a Van Gujjar who'd received land in Gandikhatta, it would probably happen there. The sense of suspense was even more acute than it had been during the days before reaching the fork at Naugaon, only this time there was no decision to make. Everything depended upon the whim of the rangers at the gate.

I hauled water with Appa and Mariam, then was sent on a mission to poke around, find the local grain mill and bring back a few kilos of atta; since they'd never been here before, Jamila couldn't tell me where it was. Once my chores were finished, I headed into Uttarkashi's main bazaar to give myself a much-needed personal tune-up, getting a shave, devouring half of a tandoori chicken— the first meat I'd eaten in weeks—and stocking up on chocolate. I knew that after Uttarkashi, we weren't going to be near many more shops, if we made it past the forest gate. And if we were turned away, well, at least we'd have chocolate.

Talking to the other families that were camped on the terrace, we learned that, if all went well, we'd have an exceptionally long hike to reach our next camp. Dhumman looked into hiring a cargo truck to move the calves and the children again, but he couldn't find a driver who would do the job for less than 1,000 rupees, and decided it was too expensive. Everyone would have to walk—including the white bull whose feet had taken such a beating on the trail over the hills that it was now wearing booties made of burlap scraps tied up with pink ribbons.

That evening, we lay down earlier than usual to try to squeeze in a few hours of rest, but sleep did not come easily to any but the smallest of children. Everyone else was well aware that before dawn broke, they might find themselves thrust into a dire situation. On this night, their world felt particularly fragile, and they feared that within a matter of hours it might shatter.

We were up before midnight and on the road by 1 AM. The black buffaloes, camouflaged by night, advanced like a ghostly army, eerily fading in and out of sight as they moved through orange pools of light cast by street lamps, then back into darkness. We marched through a tunnel in the mountainside, then entered Uttarkashi, passing the shuttered shops and the dormant bus and taxi stands of the main market. We kept going for several more miles, then crossed the bridge into Gangori. When we reached the small ranger post where the forest gatekeepers were stationed, it was almost 4 AM and still pitch dark.

Dhumman and Yusuf went inside to show their borrowed papers to the rangers on duty. The rest of the clan, including Alfa, continued driving the herd forward, passing beneath the metal bar that spanned the road, which was raised at just enough of an angle to walk beneath, but was clearly not wide open. Knowing that the anxieties that possessed them would be invisible to a casual observer, they forged ahead with a show of false confidence. If they looked like they were doing exactly what they were supposed to be doing, they thought, perhaps the rangers would believe them and let them pass.

It seemed to work.

After a few minutes, Dhumman and Yusuf emerged from the small office and ran to catch up with the family. They said that everything was okay, for the moment anyway. They'd been told that a ranger would go over their paperwork more thoroughly later, at a more decent hour, at their next camp, which they understood to mean that the officials here were open to negotiating. A wave of quiet relief swept through the group. They quickened their pace and didn't look back, as though doing so might inspire the rangers to change their minds.

We trekked for six or seven hours more, following the twists and turns of the tarmac alongside the Assi Ganga River, a small tributary of the Bhagirathi that sluiced between rocky, pine-forested slopes. We stopped at last on a flat, grassy spit of land at a bend in the river and set up tarpaulins among a few cedar trees.

The weather was fickle throughout the day. Blue skies were suddenly obscured by clouds, rain was chased off by the sun, the temperatures seemed to rise and fall with the flick of a switch. Once, a cloudburst hurled hail with such force that Dhumman, Bashi and Goku gathered the buffalo calves and brought them under the tarp to take shelter with the family; people and animals pressed together beneath the sheet of black plastic until the fury of the storm passed.

When the ranger arrived, he inspected the documents that had been borrowed from Kasim, and pronounced that Dhumman, Yusuf, Alfa and their families had no right to be where they were. Kanasar, he said, was part of a different ranger district, and the permit that they had did not allow them to graze their animals in this one. Dhumman explained that they were just passing through and that they'd enter the adjacent district designated in the paperwork as soon as they could. This wasn't good enough for the ranger, who said that the entire caravan had to get out of his jurisdiction immediately or face arrest.

Dhumman, Yusuf, and Alfa understood this threat for what it was and took a stroll with the ranger so they could talk in private, out of earshot of the rest of the family. Thus the bargaining began.

When it was over, Dhumman, Yusuf, and Alfa had secured a handshake deal allowing them to move through this district to Kanasar. The ranger walked away with 2,000 rupees, seven liters of milk and three kilograms of butter, plus a promise of five more kilos of butter over the next few days.

The following morning, we woke and started off later than usual. Now that we were truly in the Himalayan foothills, we didn't have to contend with brutal daytime temperatures, and now that we were no longer travelling along a major road, there was hardly any traffic to worry about. It was lovely, walking alongside the rushing creek at the bottom of a V-shaped gorge, immersed in the aroma of pine, and every so often, when the canyon turned just the right way, catching a glimpse of snow-covered peaks that rose ahead. And those, I would learn soon enough, weren't even the big mountains.

At one point, we passed a small school. The students were outside in a field playing cricket. I turned to Mariam, and said, "I bet you'd be awesome at that game."

"I was," she answered, matter-of-factly.

"What do you mean? When did you play cricket?" I wanted to know. "When RLEK ran the forest school, we used to play all the time. I was a great batswoman, and I loved it," she said. Appa, overhearing, agreed; she loved the game, too. I could only imagine how good a Van Gujjar team might have been, armed with their strength and coordination.

I'm not sure what connections were bridged inside my brain, or why, but hearing that they enjoyed playing cricket—which doesn't fit any stereotypes of the forest-dwelling nomad—triggered in me an appreciation for just how much like contemporaries my companions seemed. It was one of those moments when you suddenly notice that something you live with every day, to which you hardly pay attention, is in fact truly extraordinary. The way we interacted, the way we related on a personal level, felt entirely familiar, entirely modern. Despite their being illiterate and living in ways that could be described as primitive, I never felt like I was talking to people from another era. Sure, our points of reference were different and the content of our conversations might bear little resemblance to the things I might talk about with friends back home; but the *style* of our conversations was very similar. In fact, I found the flow between us, as expressed in tone and body language and laughter, much easier and less awkward than I did with some Americans from different cultural, religious, or political milieus.

While I was thinking about this, it occurred to me that another, more concrete, thing that I had taken for granted but which also had a huge impact on my relationship with my Van Gujjar family was that they never drank alcohol. I'm not moralistic about drinking, but I've had enough unpleasant experiences in countries around the world, including my own, to know that drunks can be unpredictable, belligerent, and incredibly annoying. I was glad I didn't have to deal with trying to manage boozed-up companions day in and day out on the migration. If chai with fresh buffalo milk and a heavy dose of sugar was the strongest thing we drank, that was fine with me.

We hiked almost all the way into Sangam Chatti, the village at the end of the road, but before we got there, most of us veered off to the right, crossed the Assi Ganga, and struck out on a footpath into the forest. Dhumman, Alfa, Mir Hamza, and a couple of Yusuf's sons went on into Sangam Chatti to pick up supplies from one of the handful of shops that served the isolated hamlets scattered beyond it in the mountains.

While in the village, Dhumman placed a call to Dehradun. Whispers of rumours he'd heard for the past couple of days were now confirmed: the forest department had reversed its decision and opened Govind National Park to the nomads.

Firoz, the Van Gujjar whose family had been stranded on the road for about two weeks, was finally on his way up to his meadow. Dhumman was glad to hear it, but by now it would be impossible for his own family to go there this year. At this point, they were one hundred percent committed to Kanasar.

Sometime over the next few weeks, Dhumman, Yusuf, and Alfa would have to make their way over to the Gangar area to pay their annual grazing taxes, even though they wouldn't be using their meadows that summer. It was crucial, they felt, to make it look like they had been there, if only on paper, so park authorities couldn't accuse them of voluntarily abandoning their traditional pastures, then use that as a reason for banning them in the future. They knew that as far as the government was concerned, whatever was written into the paperwork would be treated as more real than whatever had actually happened on the ground.

8

MANY DAYS TO DODI TAL

O nce we crossed the Assi Ganga, we set out on a trail that was as steep as a staircase. Huffing and puffing as we climbed up a lushly forested hillside, we put the river further below us with each step. We moved slowly, by necessity, following the sharply cut valley upstream, as it curved to the east.

We were done with the road. From here on, we would travel by footpath, working our way deeper and higher into the mountains.

After about fifteen miles, we would reach Dodi Tal, a small lake popular with trekkers, which is said to be the birthplace of Lord Ganesha. From there, we would make a final push for six more miles, up and over a high pass, to the meadow at Kanasar, where the families would spend the summer at about 12,500 feet above sea level. Though there was a well-travelled recreational hiking route to Dodi Tal carved into the northern slope of the Assi Ganga Valley, we avoided it, preferring the solitude of the southern side, where the unmaintained trails were rarely used.

Had we needed to, we could have covered the final twenty-one miles of our journey in just a few days. But now that we were immersed in the forest, my companions were in no rush to reach the end of the trail. The dangers and discomforts of camping on the roadside were gone, and more importantly, we were surrounded by fodder for the animals. While there was some motivation to move quickly to avoid being hassled by the rangers who wanted us out of their district, that concern was far outweighed by an even more compelling reason to travel slowly: due to the altitude at Kanasar, we had to give the grass up there a little more time to grow. It would have been a big mistake to arrive too early, only to find nothing for the buffaloes to eat.

With our newly-relaxed pace, we slept until sunrise, hiked for a few hours, then made camp again. Though distances were relatively short, they were physically gruelling. Often, the trail was sloppy with mud or broken up by rocks. Sometimes we had to descend a couple hundred feet, only to climb right back up again, regaining every inch we'd lost. Occasionally, we traversed tricky sections along exposed cliffs, where the earth had fallen away in landslides and the trail was hardly wide enough for the pack animals to keep their footing. Sometimes we had to ford fast-flowing streams, taking care that the children and the buffalo calves all crossed safely to the other side.

Despite these challenges, there was a magical aura to this place. With the sun filtering through the forest canopy, we moved in an ethereal world of emerald flecked with gold. The spongy moss covering ancient boulders, the grasses in a tangle like windswept hair, the vines and creepers curling over bony deadfall, the leaves shimmering, quaking on bushes and trees, the long, elegant needles crowning old, majestic pines—it was all infused with such a rich and dreamy glow, I half expected to encounter nymphs or fairies while I was out gathering firewood or fetching water from a creek.

Surrounded by woods, often shielded by trees from the open sky, it was usually impossible to get a true sense of our surroundings. Only when we'd pass through a clearing that opened up an expansive view of the valley could we appreciate the scale of the terrain we were travelling through; only then did it hit home that, compared to the landscape, we were like fleas walking across the side of an elephant.

For the first time on the migration, evenings were a time for enjoyment, rather than just for sleep. Some nights, Van Gujjars from other families that were moving through the hills came to sit and talk and share tea around our bonfire. Other nights, we entertained ourselves: I would teach my friends an American game, then they would teach me an Indian game; they would sing a Van Gujjar song, then I would sing an American song.

They especially loved listening to folk tales from around the world, perhaps because they have very few such fables of their own. "We're too busy for that kind of thing," Jamila told me, which surprised me, as I'd imagined that a culture without television would have a trove of stories told to amuse and educate. My friends quickly realized what they'd been missing, and began asking me and Namith to tell a story every night.

After five days of slowly moving upriver on the south side of the valley, we crossed the Assi Ganga and camped on a flat bench of land about ten feet above the water, on the river's northern side. When I asked Dhumman how long it would take us to get from there to Dodi Tal, he said, "Two days." It sounded like we'd be picking up the pace.

But that day, the weather took a turn for the worse. Rain fell, steady and cold. A gray mist permeated the valley. Nothing was glowing anymore. My companions wrapped themselves in woolen shawls and blankets, or wore them like capes. Either way, they got wet. Dhumman became acutely concerned that it would snow. The buffaloes, he said, couldn't tolerate freezing temperatures for long. Meanwhile, one of Yusuf's sons had gone on and scouted out the trail ahead, and returned to report that it was blocked by fallen trees and landslides. The animals would never make it up.

Dhumman, Yusuf, and Alfa dispatched a couple of men from each of their families to work on clearing the trail. While Appa, Goku, Mariam, and Sharafat collected fodder for the buffaloes, Dhumman assigned me to gather firewood. He didn't want cookfire sticks, which were just a few fingers thick—he wanted fat pieces that could burn for hours. If I'd had an axe or a saw, my job would have been substantially easier, but they didn't carry a saw, and the only axe they had was off with the trail crew. I lifted and dragged what I could, and sometimes dropped big rocks on logs that were too long for me to move, smashing the beams in two, then carrying the pieces.

Just when I thought I might have brought in enough wood, I spied a huge timber along the river's edge. I knew it was exactly what Dhumman wanted. It was so perfect—and so large—I imagined hauling it into camp would be something of a triumph. I approached it, only to realize that I could barely move it—which only increased my resolve to figure out how I could bring it in. I knew there had to be a way to maneuver it up the embankment to the campsite, if I could just apply the right kind of leverage—but also knew that if I slipped and the log rolled backward, it might end up in the river or, worse, on top of me. Eventually, after a few false starts and much cursing and sweating, I wrangled it over the lip of the hill, then moved it forward by lifting the rear end, swinging it to the front, and laying it down, then going back to the rear, swinging it to the front, and laying it down, time after time, until I finally set it down alongside the woodpile, when Jamila waved me under our thin plastic roof for some warm milk. While I'd been trying to outsmart a piece of wood, she and Salma had spread a thick layer of green pine needles beneath the tarpaulin, creating a floor that was softer, cleaner, and warmer than bare dirt, infusing our Spartan shelter with homey comfort, making a primitive situation more civilized.

Later that night, as one end of the giant log was burning in the fire that had been built at the edge of the tent, flaring and smoking in the rain, Dhumman rested his hand on my shoulder. "I like people who work hard," he said. "Everything you do is a big help to us. Thank you." His plain-spoken words struck my heart. The praise felt more fatherly than friend-like, and came from a father who didn't give praise easily. It seemed like a threshold had been crossed—not unlike the day, early in the migration, when the dog first accepted me as part of the family—but this carried much more meaning. When the dog stopped wanting to kill me, it simply meant I was no longer a stranger. With Dhumman, it had taken weeks, but I'd finally won his respect.

Down at the bottom of the valley, in a dark world saturated by freezing rain, a feeling of closeness settled over us all beneath the leaky tarp. Perhaps it was the weather, perhaps it was our weariness, perhaps it was the amount of time we had spent together—sharing food, sharing chores, sharing shelter; for the moment, anyway, as we clustered beside each other sharing the warmth of the bonfire, I felt like I belonged with this family, and they seemed to feel that I belonged with them, too. We were all in this together. Gazing at my companions, who were partly illuminated by the flames, partly invisible in the shadows of the night, I wondered what it would be like to truly be a part of this family—and I wondered, if I was single and unattached, without my own little family back home, if I might try to find out. What would it be like, I mused, to marry a Van Gujjar?

Since even in a hypothetical universe I had no interest in child marriage, my thoughts turned to Appa as the only available possibility. She and I had an easy, natural connection and our friendship continued to grow day by day. She was smart and kind, funny and incredibly competent. I'd seen her in situations that were stressful and intense, as well as those that were domestic and mundane, and regardless of the circumstance, I was always happy to be around her—and the feeling seemed mutual. What's more, over the course of the migration, she seemed to become even more beautiful than she was at the start.

I wondered: if I proposed to her, would she accept? Of course, marrying me would solve all of her biggest problems—we would settle her divorce, she would have a new husband, *and* she could remain with her own family (though, as I envisioned it, we would live in a separate hut). For my part, if I didn't think too deeply about it, it was easy to be seduced by the romantic idea of retreating from the modern world and beginning a new life in the forest, with an attractive woman whom I liked and respected. Or perhaps we would spend half the year with her family in India, and half the year in America . . .

If it sounds like I might have been getting a little carried away, well, I didn't really get that far. The idea was so outlandish that even my imagination couldn't run with it much beyond a Bollywood-like fantasy of Appa and me living together in the jungle in blissful simplicity: I would teach her English as we gathered fodder, she would teach me Gujari while she cooked, then, while milking buffaloes, we would break into an elaborate musical number; singing and dancing together around the animals, we would inexplicably find ourselves wearing colorful changes of clothing, as hundreds of nomads emerged from the trees, dancing and clapping in the background.

In reality, even if Appa would consider marrying someone who was neither from her tribe nor of her religion—which is a very big "if"—I knew I had none of the skills, strength, or experience, to be a good Van Gujjar. I couldn't climb trees; I'd never delivered a newborn calf; I was totally unfamiliar with the uses and dangers of the various plants in the forest. I'd be worthless as a husband and worth even less as a father, unable to teach our children anything they'd need to know to survive as buffalo herders. I was so obviously unfit to head a nomadic household, even my daydream of it deflated before it could get off the ground.

It was just as difficult to imagine bringing Appa back to America. So far from her family, without the constant companionship that was a fundamental element of her life, she would be miserable. Sure, her life would be much easier in many ways, but it would also be a whole lot emptier.

Any way I looked at it, it would have been completely impossible. Which, really, was just as well, since I wasn't single and unattached.

On this night of such miserable weather, we played no games and told no stories, but went to bed early. Everyone in the family slept side-by-side, huddled together under blankets that they shared for warmth. Despite how close to them I had become, I slept nearby but distinctly apart; rather than sharing their blankets with them, I buried my head inside my sleeping bag, trying to keep myself warm. Some boundaries, I felt, were better left intact.

The weather the next morning was marginally better, with clouds overhead and fog hanging in the valley, but no rain. The trail crew went back out to finish clearing the route, for until the trail was passable, we weren't going anywhere. I hung around the camp, and spent some time chatting with Bashi, the eleven-year-old. Usually busy with the buffalo calves or doing chore after chore after chore, for some reason she had more free time on this day than usual. She was a sweet and gentle kid, and when I asked her which of the buffaloes was her favorite, she paused, then said she loved them all the same—seemingly concerned that if she named one, she'd hurt the feelings of the others. Still imagining what it would be like to live as a Van Gujjar, though with a very different scenario in mind than the night before, I asked her what my two-and-a-half-year-old son, Lucas, would need to know if he was going to learn to be a buffalo herder.

"First, he would need to know what to feed them, depending on how old they are," Bashi said. She described the nutritional timeline of their buffaloes: how the calves feed solely on their mother's milk for the first two weeks of life, after which they are also given leaves. When they get a little older, grass is mixed in with the leaves, and milk is mostly cut out, though they're still allowed to have a little as a treat—and to help the mama buffaloes continue to lactate.

"Would it be better for him to start out herding calves or full-grown buffaloes?" I asked, sure she would say the babies.

But she surprised me with her answer, both for its content and its thoughtfulness. "Whichever he seems to understand better. Some kids think the adults are easier to work with, but others like the calves more. Once he gets used to working with the ones he understands best, then he can learn to work with the others." I said that Bashi herself seemed to be drawn to the calves, and she smiled. "They're sort of like little sisters," she said.

By early afternoon, the trail was usable, if barely. Concerned that the pack animals, which were in varying states of injury and exhaustion, might not survive the strenuous climb to the next camp if they were fully loaded, it was decided that we would make the move in stages. A group of us would shuttle up whatever items we could carry in our hands, on our backs, or on our heads. The buffaloes would follow. Then, most of us would retreat back down the trail and wait until the next morning to move the main camp.

I filled my backpack with some of the family's food supplies and set off with the others who'd been pressed into service as porters. It wasn't long before we reached the first of several trees that had fallen across the path, and I understood why we'd had to wait before we could go forward. The downed trees were so big that they couldn't be lifted or moved, so the trail crew had had to chop sections out of them, creating gaps in the trunks that were large enough for the buffaloes and the pack animals to walk through. Seeing that several trees had diameters larger than truck tires, I was stunned that my friends had been able to cut clear through them with hand axes.

The trail was a slick and narrow ramp that wended over earthen ramparts, across boulder fields, and through fire-scarred groves that were black and gray with charred wood and ash. At times, the path vanished completely, and we had to scramble up the side of the canyon until we found it again. By the time we reached our destination—a wide, natural terrace called Manji, where there was plenty of room for the tents and the animals, not far from the main trekking trail to Dodi Tal—I was drenched with perspiration.

But there was no time to rest. Within minutes of our arrival, a cold rain began to fall. We quickly pitched a makeshift tarp to cover the family's belongings and started a fire by drenching some sticks in kerosene, then lighting them. I stayed at the tarp with all of the stuff we'd hauled, while everyone else went back down to help bring up the buffaloes.

In the persistent drizzle, I scouted around under trees and bushes for dead wood that wasn't too damp. I stacked it under the lip of the tarp and, once I had a substantial pile, hunkered down inside the shelter myself. I changed into a dry, long-sleeved shirt and put on my rain jacket. I fed the fire, munched on biscuits and chocolate, breathed deeply, and savored this moment of solitude. When living with a close-knit group of people 24/7 for weeks on end, no matter how much you like them, time alone becomes a precious commodity.

The temperature continued dropping. It felt like it was going to snow. When the first group of buffaloes arrived, my friends ran over to the fire, loaded it with the wood I'd gathered, and thrust their frigid hands towards the flames with fingers spread. People were cold and wet but, circled close around the fire, spirits were high, and boisterous conversation was punctuated with laugher. Since none of the patriarchs had reached the bivouac yet, I pulled out a packet of *bidis* I carried—mainly for the purpose of giving away as a gesture of friendship to other Van Gujjars. Now, everyone indulged, including Mariam and Goku. "You smoke?!" I asked the teenage girls. "Just sometimes," they said. "It will help keep us warm." I laughed. Over the next few days, I saw a number of the women and girls smoking, and all said it helped them tolerate the cold—they may have believed it, but it was also clearly an excuse to partake in an illicit pleasure. None of the children in the family, male or female, of any age, ever smoked in front of their fathers. Even Chamar, who was in his late twenties, was the father of four kids, and loved puffing on bidis, never dared light up if Yusuf was around.

Soon enough, Yusuf was around. He arrived with Dhumman and Alfa, bringing up the buffalo calves. As they moved in for some warmth, their sons gathered more wood and built another fire, a huge one with flames that shot up higher than their heads. Despite the weather, which hovered somewhere between miserable and dangerous, the mood became downright festive. Some of the bigger little kids—like Salma, Rustem, and Karim—had come up to Manji, too, so there would be fewer children to manage on the trail in the morning, and they were running around in the mist, impervious to the wet, freezing air. I began to doubt that the Gujari language had a word for "hypothermia."

Those of us who were heading back down to the other camp had to beat the darkness. Thanks to the rain, the trail was now soupy with mud. Traction was impossible, and to the guys I descended with, it was also irrelevant. They raced at thrilling speeds, colluding with gravity to hurtle downhill while somehow keeping their spinning feet under control. With years of experience as a wilderness guide, I am no novice in the backcountry, but I had no chance of keeping up; compared to them, I probably looked like I'd never stepped off a sidewalk in my life.

When I reached the bottom, they were waiting for me. We walked into camp together, just before dusk. From my knees down, it looked like I was made of chocolate. I got as clean as I could while Appa brewed tea, then we drank together by the fire.

The rain continued through the night, rapping like a snare drum on our thin plastic shelter. Up at Manji, where Dhumman, Salma, and some of the others had stayed, it was snowing.

The skies cleared as morning broke. By the time we started climbing, the sun shone above, beaming brightly through the tree cover. The light was crisp and clean and everything in the forest snapped into ultra-sharp focus. The trail, however, was still a mess. The wisdom of shuttling part of the camp up the previous day soon became apparent: one of the pack horses slipped and fell and, for all its heaving, couldn't lift itself up while weighed down by its saddlebags. As quickly as they could, Hamju and Chamar freed the horse from its burden. It rose awkwardly to its feet and gingerly followed the caravan up the path, while Hamju hoisted the saddlebags onto his own back and continued climbing up the side of the canyon. With every step, the muscles in his thighs and calves bulged with the strain of supporting a load meant for a horse.

I can't say exactly how far Hamju hauled the saddlebags, but he carried them for at least a half-hour or forty-five minutes, up the very steepest part of the very sloppy trail. Watching him, I was doubly amazed—in part at the fact that he was, at this point, literally stronger than our horses, but also at the fact that, even after weeks of living with them, my friends still had the ability to amaze me.

Our campsite at Manji was in a flat clearing nestled between a grassy hill dotted with boulders and a dense forest of tall pines. A creek flowed nearby, and we were just far enough off the trail that we were invisible to hikers heading to Dodi Tal. It was obvious that we weren't going to reach the little lake ourselves in the two days' time that Dhumman had predicted three days earlier.

Namith was growing impatient with the rate of our progress, or lack thereof. He was tired, and he'd already been on this journey longer than he'd originally signed up for, since when he agreed to translate for me, we both thought that we'd be making the substantially shorter migration to Gangar. Now, he was seriously considering bailing out and heading home to Dehradun. He asked Dhumman how many days it would take to reach Dodi Tal from where we were currently camped. Dhumman, once again, said, "Two." Namith digested this new information in silence, and with more than a little bit of scepticism.

Had we wanted to, we could have made it to Dodi Tal in just a few hours, but there was no incentive to do so. If it had snowed where we were, it had surely snowed at Kanasar, further setting back the clock for our ascent to the high meadow. Dhumman thought it made sense to take advantage of this new delay by re-stocking our supplies from the shops at Sangam Chatti, the village at the trailhead—which we had passed about a week earlier—before moving forward. From Manji, it would be possible to make the round-trip to Sangam Chatti in a single day, whereas if we waited until we reached Dodi Tal or Kanasar to resupply, the journey down and back would surely be too long to cover during daylight. Since we were in no rush to move forward, we would lay over at Manji the following day while a supply run was made—and Dhumman asked me to go with the team that would make it.

In normal circumstances, when Van Gujjars need to restock their foodstuffs during summer, a couple of people descend with the horses and bulls, and the animals haul everything back up to the *bugyals*. Our horses and bulls, however, were much too weak to make the trip, so Gamee, Hamju, Sharafat, Chamar, Mariam, Goku, and I descended without them, leaving at dawn and hoofing it ten miles down to Sangam Chatti, along the main Dodi Tal trail. Compared to the way we had come, this well-maintained route was like a superhighway; it was steep but it was direct, with no obstacles and firm footing.

From one of the dry goods shops, we purchased what we needed: *atta*, rice, tea, sugar, potatoes, and spices. While waiting for the clerk to bring everything to the counter, I phoned home on the shop's land line. There had been no mobile connectivity since we'd passed through Uttarkashi ten or twelve days earlier, making this by far the longest I'd gone without speaking to my girlfriend and our son since the start of the migration. She answered, surprised to hear from me out of the blue, glad to hear I was safe after my extended silence. I tried to explain where I was and what I was doing, but I only managed to talk in scrambled circles about the weather and how beautiful the landscape was and how it was taking longer than I anticipated to reach Kanasar. When it came to telling her about our life on the trail, there was simply too much to say in a short phone call about a scenario that was so completely foreign to her that I hardly knew where to begin, and ended up feeling like I was trying to describe life on an alien planet for which words hadn't yet been invented. But it didn't really matter. I just wanted to hear her voice and listen to my son and let him know that, yes, I still existed and would see him again before too long. When I hung up, I forked over the 150 rupees that I owed, which seemed to my friends like a stunning amount of money to pay for a phone call, but to me seemed like a bargain.

When it came time to divide up the supplies, Goku and I split a sack of *atta* between us. It weighed 100 pounds. I put my half in my empty pack, while she carried hers wrapped in a shawl that rested on her back but was supported by her head. Once everyone was ready, we set off. The haul back to Manji was a beast. The trail gained about 6500 feet in elevation, and I felt like I might as well have been carrying a giant rock in my bag. Somewhere around the eighth mile of our ascent (which was the seventeenth mile of the day), Goku and I found ourselves trailing far behind everyone else. Sometimes I mustered my willpower and surged ahead of her, other times she passed me. (By this time, at least, the painful abscess on her foot had healed.) We struggled onward together with a sense of camaraderie, and I was glad to see that after weeks of intense physical activity, I was now about as strong as a fourteen-year-old Van Gujjar girl.

We loped into camp side-by-side, like fellow warriors emerging from battle, battered but victorious.

With every muscle in my body exhausted, I slept well that night. When I woke in the morning, I was surprised to find that no one was packing up. "We're staying here another day," Jamila said. "The horses and bulls need more rest." Though it was clearly a sensible decision, I couldn't help being disappointed. I was eager to move forward and was beginning to feel like Charlie Brown trying to kick a football—only the football was Kanasar, and Dhumman was Lucy Van Pelt, always pulling it away after holding it in front of me. Namith, who had doubted Dhumman's most recent predictions about our progress from the instant he uttered them, gave me a look that said, "I told you so."

Gamee came over to us and said he was going to go all the way up to Kanasar that very day, in just a few minutes, to scout out the situation at the meadow. He wanted to see if there was any grass growing yet, and what kind of condition the huts were in. He invited me go with him, and I instantly said "Sure!" It sounded better than hanging around camp when I was in the mood to move—and I could bring back pictures, so the rest of the family could see for themselves how things looked at Kanasar.

We travelled light and fast. I carried my camera, some water, my rain gear, my polypro shirt, and the few chapatis that Jamila had given us for lunch. Gamee carried his *lathi*.

An hour-and-a-half later, we were walking alongside the waters of Dodi Tal. A round pool the color of smoky topaz, it was more a pond than a lake. Trout darted through the translucent shallows, disappearing as they flitted into the opaque depths toward the center. A small white temple sat on one shore, and a few shack-like shops offered hot chai, Maggi noodles, and a limited selection of candy to hungry trekkers. Positioned where it was, tucked into the forest with no scenic vistas, the lake itself failed to impress me. I could understand why some people might want to hike all the way up to Dodi Tal to visit Ganesha's birthplace, but the aesthetic rewards alone didn't seem worth the effort of a purely recreational trip unless one is continuing past it, to Kanasar.

Beyond Dodi Tal, a trail wends its way through a tight, rocky canyon, criss-crossing a stream numerous times. It then switch-backs up the walls of a steep, treeless bowl, climbing nearly 3,000 feet over a pass on a high, exposed ridge. From there, it's an easy mile-long jaunt to Kanasar over open meadows, with staggering views of the snow-covered, 20,722' summit of Bandarpunch towering above the scenic canyon carved by the waters of the Hanuman Ganga.

The weather was perfect, and we kept a quick and steady pace even as we ascended the imposing face of the open bowl, our bodies moving as if on auto-pilot all the way up to the pass and onward across the *bugyals*.

When we reached the camp at Kanasar, we found two huts— one large and one small. Gamee inspected them, inside and out. The smaller one had obviously been used to house buffaloes. It needed a good cleaning and a little bit of roof work, but it wasn't in bad shape. The big *chhappar*, however, wouldn't be habitable without major renovations. The walls, made of sticks and long strips of pine bark, needed to be rebuilt in numerous places. The kitchen hearth would have to be entirely reconstructed. The roof was just a bare skeleton of tree limbs, with nothing covering the rafters that could actually shield the inside from rain and snow. It was a real fixer-upper.

I took pictures of the dwellings, to give my friends an idea of the extent of the renovations that would be required, and of the surrounding area, so Dhumman, Yusuf, and Alfa could gauge when the meadows would be robust enough to support their herds.

Gamee and I sat outside the big *chhappar* and ate our chappatis in silence, basking in the warmth of the sun, soaking in the Himalayan views—the soaring ridgeline of Bandarpunch rising in a stark white silhouette against the sapphire sky; a majestic topography of corrugated, crumpled rock unrolling beneath the snowy peak; and far below that, the river curving in a sensual arc from its glacial headwaters, through a gentle grassy basin, then vanishing into a rugged chasm framed by sheer cliffs. Though I knew we needed to turn around soon to reach our camp before dark, the view was so sweet my eyes didn't want me to leave. It was hard to imagine a more beautiful place to spend the summer.

Back down at the camp, I found Appa at work in a haze of acrid smoke. After so many miles of walking, everyone's shoes were riddled with holes and cracks and other symptoms of wear. Appa took the worst-damaged, cut them into pieces and then, with the glowing metal of a *patal* blade that was heated in a fire, she melted them onto the shoes that were worth fixing, patching holes and reinforcing worn-out spots. We greeted each other familiarly and were beginning to make small talk when Dhumman came over and asked to see the photos from Kanasar.

I pulled out my camera and turned it on. The family clamored for a glimpse of the LCD screen. They wanted to look at the images over and over, asking me to zoom in on the landscape shots so they could assess the state of the grass. The meadows, all agreed, were not quite ready for the buffaloes. The grass needed a little more time to grow.

That conclusion, I think, sealed Namith's decision to depart, though perhaps he had already made up his mind. As it turned out, Mustooq had decided the time had come for him to return to the Shivaliks, feeling that his wife and two young sons had been stuck there without him, tending to his sick father, long enough. Namith and Mustooq would leave together, the next morning, accompanying each other as far as Uttarkashi. Namith asked if I was ready to go, too.

I didn't even consider it.

Though my ability to communicate would obviously suffer without Namith in the picture, by this time I knew everyone in the family so well that basic interactions had become second nature and didn't require any interpretation in either direction. My Hindi vocabulary had grown a little, too, and my friends were always patient when I paused to flip through a phrasebook. While I did spend many hours with Namith on most days, I also spent many hours without him, doing things like shuttling the family's belongings up to Manji, or going on the supply run to Sangam Chatti, or hiking up to Kanasar. Recalling the days I'd spent without a translator along the Asan River, and how worthwhile they had been, only reinforced my conviction that there was no reason to leave now. Of course I would have preferred for Namith to stay, but I didn't try to talk him out of going. I knew the trip had been a strain on him, that he had physically pushed himself beyond anything that he'd expected, and that, with the glacial pace of our progress, he was losing interest in the endeavor. Everyone understood his reasons for leaving, and we all knew that if he didn't really want to be there, it would be best if he wasn't.

Shortly after sunrise the next morning, while the air was still cold enough to condense into plumes of steam every time we exhaled, we loaded up the horses and bulls. We climbed out of our secluded nook in the forest and up onto the main trail to Dodi Tal. There, we all paused, bidding farewell to Mustooq and Namith with heartfelt handshakes, wishing one another safe journeys. I promised to call Namith when I got back to Dehradun, to fill him in on whatever happened next, and to pay him what I still owed him. In that case, he said with a smile, he'd look forward to meeting again soon. We laughed, then we went our separate ways. I felt like I was saying goodbye to a friend, but I wasn't sad to see him leave.

The walking was easy and the weather was good, so I was surprised when, once again, we stopped short of Dodi Tal, trying to squeeze an extra day out of the route. There was little flat ground to be found, so Alfa and his family pitched their tents about a mile away from the small spot where Dhumman and Yusuf set up. Both camps were tucked just off the trail, lightly camouflaged behind stands of leafy trees.

From this day on, food was strictly rationed. Though we had just stocked up a few days earlier, Jamila and Roshni became hyper-conscious about our level of consumption, hoping to stretch their supplies as long as possible before having to head back down the mountain for more. We were allowed two chapatis for breakfast, two for lunch, and two for dinner— smeared with either butter and ground chili or butter and sugar. A small bowl of buffalo milk could help take the edge off our hunger pangs, but as the days passed, we became accustomed to living with a growl in our bellies most of the time. At their traditional pastures at Gangar, Appa told me wistfully, they'd never had to ration like this, since those meadows were only a few quick miles from a village where they could buy flour, rice, and other essentials.

After helping Goku and Mariam haul water from a creek that was large enough to be spanned by a cement footbridge, I hiked back down the trail to Alfa's camp. Word had come through another group of Van Gujjars travelling along the same route that one of Alfa's close relatives, who now lived at the settlement in Gandikhatta, had passed away. The family would be gathering in Gandikhatta for mourning, and Alfa needed to be there, despite the massive inconvenience of leaving the mountains. He was going to start off on his days-long journey that afternoon, so I wanted to say goodbye, thinking I would be gone by the time he returned.

When I reached their tents, Alfa's wife Sakina welcomed me warmly, and their teenage daughter Khatoon immediately stoked the fire and put on a pot of tea. Niko, the eldest son, came over from under his tent to join us, leaving his wife, who wasn't feeling well, to rest quietly alone. Their three small children, wearing balaclavas and layers of dirty sweaters, toddled and crawled around us beneath the plastic sheet, ultimately settling down in someone's lap or clinging to someone's neck or arm. I'd spent plenty of time around Alfa's family, since they often camped right alongside Dhumman and Yusuf, and we usually travelled together; now that they were further away than shouting distance, it felt like I'd gone to pay a visit to long-time neighbors who had just moved across town.

Sitting there with the steamy sweetness of chai wafting over my face every time I raised the ceramic bowl to drink, I suddenly noticed how normal all this seemed to me—and how crazy it was that it all seemed normal. After all, I was travelling with nomadic water buffalo herders in the Himalayas and could walk between their camps, sit down under their tents, and be greeted not as a stranger, but as a friend. Once, this scenario would have been a dream that I could only hope would come true. But now this absurdly extraordinary experience had come to feel about as special as going to the post office. Realizing this, I almost started laughing out loud. How quickly the fantastic becomes mundane!

Alfa arrived just after we'd finished our chai. I shook hands with him and looked one last time into his piercing, crystal-blue eyes. Our goodbyes were quick—partly because of the language barrier, partly because he was eager to start his descent—but conveyed a mutual sense of gratitude for having had the unlikely opportunity to know one another.

Clouds had swept in, obscuring the sky, casting a drab pallor over the forest. Walking back along the trail, a light drizzle bounced off my umbrella. I picked up my pace, hoping to get to shelter before the storm turned mean. When I got there, I found a few of my friends waiting for me, so I could break out my first-aid kit. At this point, nearly everyone had small wounds and minor injuries. Goku and Hamju each had cuts on their hands, which I cleaned and bandaged, though I was sure the bandages wouldn't last long, since my patients weren't going to stop doing their chores. Mariam had stepped on a sharp pine needle that had broken off under the skin on the ball of her foot. Squeeze around it as she might, it wouldn't pop up to the surface. With a safety pin and tweezers, I was eventually able to dig it out, which gave her great relief. I was surprised that the pine needle had managed to pierce her foot; her soles were so rough, they looked like they were covered in tortoise skin.

❧

When we reached Dodi Tal the next day, our caravan marched past the little row of shops and around the water's edge to the far side of the lake—which took perhaps two minutes. Hiking on for another few hundred yards, we followed the shallow creek that fed into the lake, crossing it a couple of times, until we reached a grassy clearing surrounded by forest on three sides, with the creek and a fractured cliff face on the fourth. At ten thousand feet above sea level, we camped just below the tree line, and just below the start of a tight box canyon from which the creek emerged. There was enough room for Dhumman's and Yusuf's families, plus their animals. Now, instead of two tents, three had been pitched; Gamee and Akloo had set one up for their little family after tensions had flared between Akloo and Roshni. Alfa's family, now led by Sakina and Niko, had stopped along the trail about a quarter-mile before Dodi Tal. They'd decided to aim for a meadow slightly south of Kanasar, so as not to overgraze the area, and it was here that our routes would diverge.

This was our last stop before Kanasar, which was only six miles away. Despite everyone's desire to get there and start settling in for the summer, the weather was too fickle for us to move forward. Intermittent bursts of sunshine were quickly obscured by clouds, which, depending on their mood, might shower us with rain or pelt us with hail. Camped where we were, the weather was merely an inconvenience—but it would have made the fully-exposed climb up and over the pass to Kanasar extremely dangerous, perhaps deadly. We had no choice but to wait for it to clear.

Our Dodi Tal days moved to a relaxed rhythm—at first, anyway. There was plenty of fodder growing in the grassy meadows along the fringe of the forest, both down near the lake and up beyond our camp, where the narrow canyon opened up into a bowl-like basin at the bottom of the pass. The buffaloes still needed to be watched while they grazed, but since there were no farmers' fields to protect, that required little more than keeping one's eyes open. The sole imperative was to make sure they didn't eat any rhododendron leaves, which buffaloes find delicious, but which are poisonous enough to sicken and kill even these large beasts.

Since Dodi Tal was a popular destination for hikers, we encountered a couple of organized trekking groups there. They were composed mainly of teenagers who had signed up for Himalayan adventure trips. One group was from Delhi, the other was from around Mumbai and Pune. Occasionally, they would pass through our camp, and the adult leaders might stop to chat and have some tea. (Since they spoke English, they translated for me a number of times, as did another independent trekker who I met, so if you begin to wonder how I managed to have some of the more detailed conversations that took place over the next few days, I had help.)

On the day that one of these groups first arrived, I happened to be wandering down to Alfa's family's camp, so I watched as the teenaged trekkers trudged up the trail towards the lake. They wore jeans and t-shirts, or maybe sweatshirts, with some of the girls wearing kurtas. Their feet were clad in hiking boots or athletic shoes. They carried small day packs, since their large bags were being hauled up by porters and mules. And they were struggling, moving slowly and with great effort, as though lead weights were strapped to their ankles. Every hundred yards or so, they stopped to rest. I spoke with a few of them during one of their many breaks, and they all agreed that they'd never done anything so physically demanding in their lives. They were very friendly and, to their credit, they persevered and made it to the lake. But I couldn't help noticing the irony of the circumstances.

These young folks were living one version of the modern Indian dream—they were obviously well educated, and came from families that could afford to send them on a recreational trip into the mountains of Uttarakhand. My Van Gujjar friends, on the other hand, were illiterate forest dwellers who lived on the margins of society, far from any version of the modern Indian dream. Yet here, on the side of a mountain, their roles were reversed in a way that seemed to reveal something important, though I have a hard time articulating exactly what that is.

Compared to the trekkers, my friends seemed to have super-powers. They were strong and confident, exuding a competence and physical grace that conveyed an aura of nobility; despite their natural humility, it was easy to believe that they might have been descendants of that princess from centuries ago. The trekkers, on the other hand, looked weak, fragile even, evoking the kind of compassion you might feel for a starving puppy. I had no doubt that five-year-old Salma could hike these teenagers into the ground.

Something about this contrast reminded me of the *bhopas* of Rajasthan, who recite oral epics for hours on end, night after night, completely from memory, until the entire story is told—and how those *bhopas* who learn to read have a diminished capacity to remember these poems, even if they've known them for years, and how their children, if schooled, can never memo-rize them completely. For some reason, acquiring the ability to read—which almost everyone agrees is a good, if not essential, skill to have—re-wires the mind so it can no longer perform such extreme feats of memory.

Reflecting on this as I witnessed the group of relatively privileged teenagers struggle up the trail, I began to wonder about the ways in which modern comforts, modern lifestyles, and especially modern technologies are eroding our mental and physical capabilities. I wondered how many of the things we do now without thinking twice will seem extraordinary, if not impossible, fifty years hence.

❧

On our third day at Dodi Tal, Dhumman left our camp late in the morning, carrying a full load of fresh milk in the metal backpack-container. He hiked all the way down the trail to Sangam Chatti, then caught a bus to the main bazaar in Uttarakashi. He sold the milk there and bought materials that the family would need up at Kanasar, including sheets of plastic to cover the roof of the old hut, whose state of disrepair was clearly evident in the photos I'd taken of it. We knew he'd be away overnight, and for most of the following day. While he was gone, the accident occurred.

9

THE STORM

S wirling gray clouds swallowed the mountaintops. A cold rain fell in surges, hard and heavy one minute, a light patter the next. Pearls of water dripped through holes in the ceiling of our tent, onto the aromatic bed of green pine needles that had been spread on the ground beneath it. The campfire burning nearby sputtered and smoldered, producing more smoke than flame.

Early that morning the skies had been clear, raising our hopes that the bad weather that had besieged us had finally broken. If we were lucky, we'd be able to tackle the final leg of our journey the next day. With this in mind, after the buffaloes were milked, Jamila asked a few of us to shuttle some of the family's belongings all the way up to the hut at Kanasar, then return. She felt that some of the bulls and horses were still too worn out to carry full loads up and over the three-thousand-foot pass that stood between us and the meadow we had to reach, and anything we could haul in advance would help.

Carrying as much as we could, Gamee, Appa, Sharafat and I followed the trail along the creek, through the tight, rocky canyon and out into the treeless bowl at the base of the pass. As we began to ascend the lower section of the bowl, which was like a ramp that became steeper and steeper, the sky darkened. We lost sight of the highest ridge, and watched as ash-colored clouds slid down the rim and into the basin. As much as we wanted to press onward, the risks of being caught in a Himalayan storm while exposed on a bare mountainside had potential consequences too grim to ignore. We cached what we were carrying among some bushes, intending to pick them up when we trekked by them the following day, and hustled back to camp through a thickening mist, arriving just as the deluge began.

After a two-chapati lunch, nearly everyone went out to watch the herds. Huddling together under umbrellas or beneath trees, they tried, unsuccessfully, to stay dry. Their plastic shoes filled with water; their woolen shawls were soaked. But they endured the storm with stoicism and mostly good humor, their own comfort less important than keeping their animals away from the deadly rhododendron.

Not feeling any particular need to get drenched myself, I stayed under the tent, catching up on some writing and talking to the women who were watching over the youngest children. Akloo, whose sculpted cheeks were loosely framed by a green-and-purple headscarf, cradled little Hasina. Appa, in a yellow polyester sweater over a green *kameez*, brushed out Salma's hair. Mariam was lying down, wrapped in a brown fleece blanket, resting but awake enough to giggle and joke with the rest of us.

It was a moment as sweet as it was mundane, with the warmth of friendship keeping us cozy beneath the flimsy piece of plastic that sheltered us from the storm.

Our relaxed banter was abruptly severed by a scream. It sounded so panicked, so distressed, I instantly thought, "Who's dead?" Appa and Mariam turned to each other with fear in their faces and simultaneously said, "Bashi!" Leaping up without bothering to put on their shoes, they dashed towards the source of the shriek. I grabbed my camera, slipped on my raincoat and shoes, and followed, while Akloo stayed under the tent with the children.

Up the canyon we ran, along the muddy trail, leaping from rock to rock to cross the churning creek, and sometimes wading through it. The sound of the rushing water was amplified by the walls of the gorge into a wild roar, heightening the sense of emergency as we raced toward the unknown disaster. After about two minutes, we met Bashi, who was sprinting towards us in tears. She could barely speak through her sobs, her whole body shaking as she tried to explain what happened. As soon as Appa and Mariam got the picture, they bolted on up the trail and I went with them, while Bashi continued running down to camp.

Bashi had been tending to the calves, as she usually did. They'd been led up the trail from the camp, to a flat bank just above the creek in the gorge that funneled runoff down from the highest ridges. Hiding from the weather, the animals clustered together at the base of a sheer cliff, instinctually seeking cover under a rock overhang, though not all of them could fit beneath it. Bashi huddled in close with the calves, knowing her presence helped calm them—and taking comfort from them as well. When the downpour temporarily tapered off, she came out from under the alcove, scrambled down the side of the bank, and crossed the creek to fetch a bundle of grass for her four-legged friends to munch on.

Suddenly, the storm burst back to life. Thunder shook the canyon. Rain exploded from the sky. At the top of the rock wall, some seventy feet directly above the young buffaloes, a flash flood became a waterfall when it poured over the precipice. In its path was a dead tree, which the surging waters lifted up and flung over the cliff's edge. Just before it struck the ground, the tree smashed into five of the buffalo calves.

Bashi saw the whole thing, and screamed with every ounce of her being. She was lucky that she'd been on the other side of the creek when the tree fell, but that didn't cross her mind. She thought only of the calves. She was terrified that they would die. She turned and ran for the tents, her bare feet splashing through frigid puddles while she cried hysterically, yelling for help. Her brothers, sisters, and cousins were already on their way.

Within minutes, eight of us had reached the site of the accident. By then, the rain had paused again. My friends surveyed the scene, taking in the size of the tree that lay splayed on the ground, then looking up to the top of the cliff and tracing its fall with their eyes. For a moment, they were frozen by disbelief, but this quickly thawed into a devastated grief for the wounded calves. Heartrending wails and sobs and shouts of protest were directed at the clouds. Their emotional response was so intense, so distressed, I couldn't imagine how they would have reacted if Bashi herself had been struck. After a minute or two of chaos, Gamee—the oldest on the scene—took on the role of incident commander and organized his brothers, sisters, and cousins for action.

Though they were focused and efficient, everyone, even the men, wept as they triaged the animals, sorting the wounded from the well, checking the injured, and building a bonfire to keep the calves warm.

The five victims were large yearlings. Two were obviously okay, their tough black hide only scraped by the tree's branches. Another two suffered blows to their bodies and seemed like they might have had internal injuries, but it was hard to tell how seriously they were hurt. The fifth was in the worst shape. Her front left leg had been crushed. A severed bone stuck out through her flesh; the hoof beneath it flopped around like it was held on by a rubber band.

Mariam warmed a burlap sack over the fire, then spread it over the back of the broken-legged yearling. Lying on the ground, she was too hurt to struggle as Gamee, Chamar, and Hamju tried to straighten her leg—which was bent at a troublingly unnatural angle—and covered the wound with a shirt and scarf. Blood dripped from the corner of the animal's mouth. She sank into deep lethargy. I'm not sure if it's possible, but it looked like tears were welling in the corners of her eyes. She seemed like she might be dying. And the rain started falling again.

I had been moved to the verge of tears myself, as much out of empathy for my distraught friends as for the injured creature. Yet, at the same time, the photojournalist in me couldn't help but recognize that I'd been thrust into a scenario the likes of which few people had ever seen, let alone photographed. I imagined the shots I could get of nomads in a Himalayan storm, weeping over their animals as they tried to care for them. My camera felt like it was jumping up and down beneath my rain jacket, begging to be taken out and used. But I couldn't bring myself to do it. The moment was so personal, so raw, I felt that taking pictures of their grief would have been intrusive and inappropriate, that their intensely emotional reaction to this sudden tragedy deserved the dignity of privacy. I imagined that a clicking camera would have introduced an element of self-consciousness at a time when my friends most needed to be themselves, without concern for how they might appear to others; and I knew that if I was in their position, I would probably not want someone snapping pictures of my moment of distress. Respecting their feelings meant more to me than any photos I might have returned with. So, resisting the temptation to shoot, I kept my camera sheathed and instead did the only useful thing I could: I sat beside the buffalo with the broken leg and gently stroked her head, trying to give her some comfort.

After about fifteen minutes, Yusuf arrived. His pointy orange beard leapt in the wind as he asked what had happened, his tone at once demanding and desperate. While listening to the story, he dropped his umbrella, knelt on the soggy ground, and examined the injured yearlings, all of which belonged to him. Upon seeing the broken leg, he slapped his hands to his forehead. Facing skyward, he ranted in anguish, uttering short, tormented outbursts, each of which ended with a pained howl seared by despair.

A few moments later, Jamila and Roshni appeared. With calm confidence, the two women took control of the situation. They ushered their children away, sending them back to camp or to the herds of adult buffaloes temporarily left unattended. I stayed to see what they were going to do. With their silver bracelets jingling, they mixed milk and turmeric powder together in a stainless steel jug and then, through a green plastic tube, poured the concoction down the throats of the three wounded yearlings to fortify them and deter infection. Jamila stoked the fire while Roshni re-warmed the burlap sack that was draped over the broken-legged buffalo's back.

Suddenly, a barrage of thunder detonated with such force that it seemed to crack the sky. Hail began to fall, violently, in balls the size of cherries. Jamila, Roshni and I ran for shelter under the rock overhang. With their scarf-covered heads tilted to the heavens, the women watched with troubled eyes as millions of ice pellets streaked through the foggy air, beating a staccato drumroll that echoed off the canyon walls. Fate, they concluded, had truly turned against them, and they keened in high-pitched tones, plaintively praying to Allah with their whole souls, pleading for mercy while accepting whatever His hand would write for them.

Of course the passion with which Jamila and Roshni prayed was fueled by more than just the accident; their fervent chants and wails seemed like expressions of all of the frustrations and difficulties they had faced throughout the migration. Perhaps worst of all wasn't even what they had endured, but what they had come to fear about the future—which was, in the simplest terms, that they had no future.

They felt like the people in the songs Van Gujjars sing, forsaken by God in a cruel world that had no place for them.

✤

That evening, Hamju and Sharafat returned to the calves with blankets and food for themselves. They would spend the night there. They concluded that the two buffaloes suspected of having internal injuries only had some bruises and would be fine. But things looked bad for the yearling with the broken leg. With an open compound fracture, I didn't see how she could survive. The only question in my mind was whether she'd be left behind to die or would be humanely euthanized, somehow.

I expected there'd be a funereal feeling in the air around camp that evening, but there wasn't. The storm was still sitting on top of us, pounding us intermittently. Between keeping an eye on the buffaloes and keeping the fires going, people were too preoccupied to wallow in emotion. Bashi had been so upset by what she'd seen and felt so guilty that it had happened on her watch, even though it clearly wasn't her fault, I had wondered how long it would take her to get over it. But by dinnertime she was clearly feeling better, the comfort given by her family quickly—if not completely—repairing her world.

Dhumman returned after dark from his mission to Uttarkashi, carrying rolls of plastic, rope, and other miscellaneous supplies. Exhausted, he sat silently and ate the chapatis that were reheated for him on the fire, while listening to the story of the accident. Finishing his chai, he quietly asked a few questions. Then he went to see Yusuf.

Sitting by the fire at Yusuf's tent, the two brothers talked for a long time. By the end of the conversation, they'd reached a decision about the yearling with the broken leg. They were going to try to save her.

***

The morning was sunny and warm, the sky pure blue. It was as though the Hindu god Indra had swept through the mountains the day before in a crazy drunken rage, which he completely forgot about when he woke up, sober and at peace.

Dhumman, Jamila, Yusuf and Roshni fine-tuned their plans. Jamila would stay at camp, while the other three, along with Yusuf and Roshni's sons, would head up the trail and try to splint the buffalo's leg. I'd go too, helping in any way I could—and hoping that, on this day, it would feel okay to take photos of what promised to be an unusual feat of veterinary improvisation. Before we left camp, Dhumman asked me to grab my first-aid kit, just in case there was anything in it that might prove useful.

When we reached the calves, we found Bashi there watching them. She sat by the wounded yearling's head, petting and kissing her, while Dhumman fashioned a splint from six thin pieces of wood and some rope, which he then put to the side.

Chamar, Gamee, and Hamju lay across the young buffalo, holding her down with the weight of their bodies. Yusuf poured turmeric powder into the gaping hole from which the bone protruded, then he and Roshni gently pulled outward on the hoof, applying traction while Dhumman jimmied the bone back in and positioned it correctly. The buffalo tried to recoil, but couldn't move.

Working slowly and meticulously, Dhumman bandaged the wound with a roll of gauze that I'd given him, then he wrapped a cloth around it, neat and tight, for padding. Over that, the wooden splint was secured as snugly as possible, first with rope, then with a long strip of duct tape from my kit. The whole procedure, including making the splint, took about an hour. It looked perfect, and could hardly have been done better in an animal hospital.

Of course, there was one problem. The buffalo still couldn't walk, and the high, steep pass still stood between us and the meadow. Perhaps, I thought, they'd stabilized the leg just to ease the yearling's pain. I couldn't see how they expected her to make it to Kanasar.

The following day, we rose before sunrise. My friends always worked efficiently when breaking camp, but on this morning the last morning of the migration—every hoisting of every bag, every cinching of every rope, was juiced with enthusiasm. The frigid, pre-dawn air seemed electrified with excitement. Everyone was eager to set eyes on the meadow, to see where the many twists and turns of this long journey had led them.

As the sky grew light, we walked out of camp and up through the narrow canyon. With the horses and bulls carrying what they could, we moved slowly, crossing the creek a number of times and navigating the tricky trail around the massive boulders that choked the gorge. We passed the spot where the accident had happened—and where the wounded yearling remained—at last emerging in the treeless bowl that we would hike up towards the pass.

The buffaloes had been moved here the previous afternoon and were waiting for us, munching on leafy bushes. They would take up the rear. Looking ahead, the trail zigzagged up a steep, grassy chute between two rocky ridges. The higher it rose, the more precarious it appeared, until it finally veered out of view far above us but still well below the pass, which we couldn't yet see. Anticipating the trouble that the pack animals would have reaching the top, their loads were reduced; we humans would carry what we could on our own backs.

And so we started up, twenty-five people, eighty-three buffaloes, and a few horses and bulls. I held Yasin's hand for a while, helping him keep his footing and imagining what it would be like to attempt this ascent with my own son, who was about the same age and quite a capable hiker, at least as far as American two-year-olds go; I smiled at the thought, missing him. When Yasin finally became too tired to walk, Jamila placed him on her shoulders.

As the trail grew yet steeper, I pushed my legs to go a little bit faster, so I could get ahead of the group and take pictures as my friends climbed toward me. From above, I could see the entire family and all the animals at once, moving up the mountainside in a serpentine formation. Men, women and teenagers carried children on their shoulders, or cooking pots and milk cans packed with household goods on their backs. Headscarves and *lungis* flapped colorfuly in the breeze. Guttural, inarticulate shouts, and the occasional smack of a *lathi*, kept the horses and bulls moving, their bells jingling in mesmerizing rhythms. With the jewel-like peaks of the 21,600' Gangotri Group gleaming on the horizon behind this caravan of nomads and their armada of big, black, horned beasts, it looked like a vision out of a dream.

The trail was narrow but in surprisingly good condition. The weather was perfect. Despite the incline and the thinning air, we made steady progress. Individuals paused for breaks here and there, to catch their breath and give their thighs a few seconds to stop throbbing, but the group as a whole kept moving forward, snaking up the mountainside. With one final push over a nearly vertical slope we cleared the pass, then sat and rested, tired and happy. From there, the rest of the walk to Kanasar felt like a victory lap. It had taken forty days; we had covered roughly 125 miles; we had gained over 11,000 feet in elevation; but we had made it.

The view from the meadow was staggering. With snow-crowned Bandarpunch towering over a dramatic canyon whose sheer walls were graced by cascading waterfalls, with alpine grasslands unfurling around us, laced with gurgling streams and fringed by evergreen forests, I found it every bit as awe-inspiring as the first time I had been there with Gamee.

After unloading the animals, we went to inspect the two tattered wooden huts that stood there, which had been built and used by other Van Gujjars in the past. The larger one had a solid frame of logs and tree limbs, but required substantial repairs. Just like any family might when moving into a fixer-upper, my friends lingered inside, dreaming about what the kitchen would look like—in this case, how they'd rebuild the hearth with mud and rocks, sculpting in some shelving to hold their cookware. But the first priorities were rebuilding the walls which had gaping holes—and the roof—which was nothing more than bare rafters. Once renovated, Dhumman's family would move into it.

The small hut needed its roof reinforced and quite a few loads of old buffalo dung removed from inside, but Gamee, Akloo, and their two kids would be able to occupy it by the end of that first day.

The rest of Yusuf's family would have to build a new hut from the ground up, which caused some grumbling among his sons, since they would be expected to do the bulk of the work on what would be a major construction job.

For now, however, everyone would continue living under sheets of black plastic until they could move into their dwellings. We quickly got to work setting up our tents, collecting firewood, and hauling water, preparing for lunch and for any weather that might move in.

Gradually, what we all knew—that this was the last stop, the end of the trail—began to seem real. As we settled into the meadow, a sense of relief settled into me, since I was now sure that I would in fact go home having seen the migration through from start to finish. Even while doing chores, I basked in that peaceful if fleeting feeling of quiet satisfaction earned by fulfilling a long-held dream. Or maybe I was simply susceptible to the transcendent beauty of Kanasar, which appeared to have the power to cast a spell of tranquility over anyone with the gift of sight.

Except I was the only one who seemed to be feeling this way. Despite the meadow's Shangri-La-like setting, something felt wrong, at least to some of my friends. After forty tough days on the trail, the brief moment of triumph they experienced upon reaching their goal faded into a palpable mood of disappointment.

Sitting beneath the lip of the tent, brewing a pot of chai, Appa summed it up for me; as we spoke, giant plumes of cumulus swept over the meadow, a fluid shroud of clouds, white and gray and gold, sometimes fraying just enough for beams of sunlight or views of the mountains to flash through. "It is more beautiful here than at Gangar," she said, "but it isn't our home." It was colder here, she continued, and higher, and there was so much work to be done before they could even move into the hut. It felt strange to be so far from a village in the summertime—and especially from the villagers whose families had been friends with her family for generations. "I love it there." She paused. "We just don't belong here."

Of course, everyone was also exhausted, both physically and emotionally, from the journey. Now that the migration was over, they could allow themselves the luxury of feeling it a little bit.

And there was something else, too. Something big. One member of the family wasn't with them. The fate of the injured calf, who'd been abandoned down below, was weighing on everyone's mind.

Fortunately, Dhumman and Yusuf had yet another plan. Early the next morning, Dhumman, his son Mir Hamza, and Yusuf's four sons headed down the mountain. When they reached the wounded yearling, they lashed her to two poles cut from slim tree trunks. Supported underneath by ropes that ran from one pole to the other, she was stabilized with ropes tied over her back. As my friends took up their positions, with one on each end of the poles, they hoisted the litter onto their shoulders. Step by grueling step, they carried the animal up, switchback after switchback, and over the pass. It was a labor worthy of Hercules. The buffalo was so heavy and the trail so steep that the men had to work on a rotation system, allowing some to rest while others carried. I willingly lent my shoulders to the effort, but found I could only lift the animal's front end, since the rear weighed so much more. A few times, we simply had to stop, lay the yearling down, and regain our strength before continuing on.

I had never in my life seen anything like this—a buffalo being carried through the Himalayas like a queen on a palanquin. Though I knew my companions well by this time, I was stunned that they would go to such lengths to save one relatively small member of their herd. They didn't do it because the yearling was worth much financially; they did it because they love their buffaloes. They did it out of the intrinsic sense of responsibility they have for their animals. They did it because they are Van Gujjars.

Upon reaching the meadow, hours after her unusual journey began, the yearling was clearly relieved to be back on the ground. With a little bit of help, she stood, and even gingerly hobbled a few steps. By the time they would descend in the fall, Dhumman said, her broken bone should be healed enough for her to walk down to the Shivalik Hills on her own four feet.

Heartened by the success of the rescue mission, grateful to have their baby back with them, a wave of optimism rippled through the camp. Perhaps their luck had turned the corner at last.

10

THE END
OF THE TRAIL

T hat night, the sheet of ice that coated the roof of our tent was thicker than the sheet of plastic that the tent was made from. Bundled into my sleeping bag, with all of my clothes either on my body or packed around me for insulation, I spent hours pulled back and forth between the exhaustion that dragged me towards sleep and the cold that shook me awake. Meanwhile, from the smoldering campfire, plumes of smoke wafted under the tarp and lingered there, filling the space with smog as thick as downtown Delhi's; whenever I opened my eyes, they stung as though they were being rubbed with nettles. When I rose in the morning, I must have looked as frayed as I felt: Goku cast an empathetic smile my way and said, "It was never this cold in Gangar." The night hadn't been easy on anyone.

Life would be greatly improved as soon as they could move into the *chhappar*, when they'd be under a real roof, protected by real walls, and could cook over a real kitchen hearth. Fixing the hut, thus, was the family's top priority. Dhumman issued orders and assigned jobs: Sharafat and Gamee—who, since the recent fallout between his wife and his mother, had been taken in under his uncle's wing of the family—would work on the roof, shoring up the beams and rafters; Jamila and Akloo would sweep up inside and stabilize the existing walls, while keeping an eye on the little kids; Mir Hamza and Bashi would take the buffaloes out to graze. Appa, Goku, and I were sent out into the forest to haul back pieces of wood with which to repair the gaping holes in the walls. Meanwhile, Yusuf's sons, except Gamee, searched out fallen trees that they could use to construct the frame of a new hut.

Appa, Goku, and I hiked across the sloping meadow, under skies bleached by wisps of cirrus. After perhaps half a mile, we dropped down into a crease in the terrain where the treeline extended up the side of the mountain, an arm-like grove reaching out from the main body of the forest below. We were looking for dead pines, the bigger the better. Their thick bark would suit our purposes perfectly. We tried to strip off pieces of it in slabs as long and as wide as possible, which we would use like boards to rebuild the walls. We hacked and pulled and pried with a spirit of playful camaraderie, turning our task into something that felt more like a game than a job. If we were lucky, we managed to free planks of bark that were about twelve feet long by two feet wide. Even the largest pieces were light enough for us to each carry a couple at a time, if they were properly balanced over our shoulders. Once we'd delivered them to the *chhappar*, we would hike back across the meadow for more.

It was work, but it was fun, and at that moment I could hardly imagine anything I'd rather be doing than foraging for wood in the Himalayan highlands with people I so thoroughly enjoyed. The pleasure, however, was bittersweet.

After one wood run, Jamila called us over to the tent for chapatis and chai. Sharafat was already there, sitting by the still-smoldering fire, eating slowly and talking to his mom. Goku, Appa, and I sat down with him. From the mouth of the tent, we had a perfectly framed view of snowy Bandarpunch. While eating the first of my two chapatis, I told my friends that I was going to have to leave the following day.

Over the course of the previous week, I'd pored over the calendar I'd drawn in the back of my notebook, trying to gauge how long I could stretch my stay in the mountains and still catch my flight back to the States. No matter how I figured it, I had finally run out of time. I didn't bother to tell my friends earlier because I knew that they would assume that any date I set in advance would be entirely flexible. As our extended journey to Kanasar had shown, they didn't operate on a fixed schedule. I knew they wouldn't believe I was leaving until I actually left.

Jamila and her kids urged me to stay with them a little longer—even just a couple more days. I laughed. "Like the two days it took to get from the Assi Ganga to Dodi Tal?" I said. And they laughed too.

If I could have stayed, I would have. Aside from simply not wanting to say goodbye yet, it would have been nice to experience daily life in the meadow once the repairs on the hut had been completed and the family settled into a more normal rhythm. But, in addition to the hassle involved in changing a plane ticket—especially from a remote location with no mobile phone service—there was the promise I'd made to my own little family to return when I'd planned, and that was something I needed to honor. It was time to start heading home.

Throughout the day, whether holding boards of bark in place while Dhumman secured them with vines, fetching water from a creek with Goku and Mariam, or simply soaking up the epic scenery, I savored every minute, knowing I had precious few remaining.

❧

Over the previous week, aware that my departure date was approaching, I'd made a point of asking Jamila and Dhumman (with the help of trekkers who could translate) about their thoughts on the migration. It had been, they agreed, a physically strenuous and emotionally nerve-wracking journey, unlike any they'd previously experienced. And it had rattled their world.

Like most Van Gujjars, they had always wholeheartedly rejected the idea of leaving the forest and settling in a village. They would lose virtually everything in their lives, including their buffalo herds, their intimate connection to the natural world, their sense of freedom, even their sense of themselves— as individuals and as a culture. "The forest is the only thing we know," Dhumman said. "We are part of it and it is part of us. It's where we belong." He said that whenever he had to spend more than a few hours in a town, he would inevitably begin to feel sick. If they could remain in the wilderness and herd buffaloes as they always had, moving freely between their traditional lands without the looming threat of eviction, they would be happy, Dhumman and Jamila concurred. But now, despite how much they loved their nomadic way of life, they had serious questions—and deep anxieties—about its viability in the future.

Forget about five or ten years down the line, they didn't even know what would happen the following spring: perhaps they'd be able to return to Gangar—or perhaps they'd be barred from Uttarakhand completely, leaving them with nowhere to take their animals in the summer. All sense of security had evaporated from their world. The fear that this provoked drove them to think that if they were offered a deal to leave the forest and settle in a village, they would probably accept it—though they each thought about it a little bit differently.

For Dhumman, settling down meant that his family would receive a house and a small plot of land in a village where some of his children could go to school—while he would continue to keep a herd of buffaloes in the forests of the Shivaliks and migrate to the Himalayas each summer. How probable or improbable his vision might have been really didn't matter, since it was more a fantasy to which he clung than a strategy he planned to execute. He just couldn't wrap his head around the idea of truly abandoning his life in the forest.

Jamila, on the other hand, seemed a bit more clear-sighted about what accepting a hypothetical settlement deal would probably mean. For her, life in the forest would be over. "Settling in a village we would lose a lot," she said. "A lot. But at least we would know where we are." The stability, the security, would be worth the trade off, she thought, if just barely.

But . . . nobody was offering them a settlement deal. The idea that they would even have this difficult choice to make was, for the moment, wishful thinking, inspired by the terrifying reality that the threat they were in fact faced with—eviction with no compensation—was much, much worse.

Based on everything I'd seen, I was convinced that the immediate goal of the forest department wasn't to kick the Van Gujjars out of Govind National Park, but to soften them up with scare tactics. By threatening to ban them completely, and acting as though they meant it, the forest department had forced the nomads to believe that they might truly lose access to their lands, perhaps forever. Yet by ultimately allowing entry to those families who hadn't found emergency alternatives, the authorities had avoided any real legal confrontation over the Forest Rights Act. As this was the third year in a row that such threats had been issued—their severity increasing with each passing year—plenty of Van Gujjars had been traumatized into thinking what once would have been anathema to them: that it might be better to live in a village than in the wilderness. While these tactics were not as blatantly abusive as those used to persuade Van Gujjars to leave Rajaji National Park, they were calculated and underhanded forms of terror nonetheless. And they were starting to work.

Along with the concrete fears that threats of eviction stirred up for Dhumman, Jamila, Yusuf, Roshni, and their fellow tribes-people—that they would be homeless and herdless—I think the threats also functioned on a more subtle level just by sowing and cultivating the idea that there might not be a future in the forest for nomads. Our hopes for the future are like balloons filled with the air of possibility. When a balloon is punctured, the air rushes out, leaving us with a shrivelled piece of rubber on a string that there's no reason to hold on to anymore. When our hopes for the future are punctured, our sense of possibility rushes out, leaving us with a shrivelled vision of what we can have, of who we can be, and we feel much less inspired to hang on to it. We can still wish for the future we dreamed of and we can grieve over its loss—but as the reality of impossibility sets in, we gradually start to imagine new futures that we slowly inflate with new hopes. By peppering the lives of Van Gujjars with profound existential insecurities, it seemed to me like the forest department was trying to pop their balloons, so they would begin to loosen their devotion to their forest world and slowly start to generate a vision, and even some hope, for another kind of life.

Perhaps, the thinking went, given enough time, the Van Gujjars would leave the forests on their own. Or, if the forest department really did want them out of Govind and other areas, and had to offer compensation packages as required by the Forest Rights Act, the nomads would more readily make a deal.

Yet despite how difficult and angst-filled the migration had been, and how uncertain the future appeared, some of my friends could neither be scared into abandoning the wilderness nor voluntarily accepting any kind of compensation in exchange for settling down. Appa, the only one in the family with actual experience of living in a village, who had told me it was like being in prison, wholeheartedly resisted the idea. "Our people have been going to the mountains forever," she insisted, passionately. "We have always migrated. Gangar is our home! No one should be able to stop us from going there." And she was not alone in thinking this way. Firoz, Dhumman's friend who had been stuck on the road waiting with his herds and his family for permission to enter Govind, was among those of the same mind.

When I asked Jamila what she thought they would do the following spring, where they would go, she shrugged and said, "We will go where it is written for us to go." I'm pretty sure she meant "by Allah"—though she might have been thinking of the forest department.

❧

After another freezing night spent half-sleeping in a smoky tent, morning broke sunny and clear. I had some chai, and as everyone went off to do whatever they needed to do—lead the buffaloes out to pasture, fetch water, work on the hut—I packed my bag for the last time. I left out a few items that I thought my friends might find useful, such as a nearly indestructible plastic water bottle, a few heavy-duty resealable plastic bags, and a couple of small carabiners. I handed them to Appa, who had stayed around the tent with Salma, Yasin, and Jamila, and she accepted them with thanks. Then I gave my polar fleece jacket to Jamila and asked her to give it to Dhumman, in case he didn't return to the tent before I had to hit the trail. She said she knew he'd like it, but she expected him back in a few minutes, so I could give it to him myself.

As a special send-off, Appa cooked up a dish made from milk, sugar, *atta*, *gud* (jaggery), and maybe a couple of other ingredients. It tasted like a sweet porridge. The smell drew Sharafat, Goku, and Gamee over from the big hut, and Akloo and her kids over from the little hut, everyone eager to share in this rare treat. For a few minutes, it was like a goodbye garden party, though instead of a manicured lawn it was held in a Himalayan meadow, and instead of being dressed in fine attire, the guests were wrapped in woolen shawls saturated with the smell of old campfire. In other words, it was hard to imagine a better kind of garden party. As spontaneously as it had begun, it was over. Sharafat, Goku and Gamee went back to working on the hut, and I walked over to Yusuf and Roshni's tent.

Not one for drawn out farewells, I tried to keep it short, but couldn't refuse a cup of tea when Roshni offered it. Beaming with warmth, she wished me a safe journey home. Yusuf urged me to come back and migrate with them again the following spring—hopefully to Gangar. He wanted me to see their real Himalayan home.

I looked at my watch. It was already after nine o'clock. I'd told myself I needed to leave by 9:30, since I had to hike about twenty miles to the trailhead at Sangam Chatti, and I wanted to get there before the daily buses to Uttarkashi stopped running sometime in late afternoon. I shook the little hands of Rustem and Djennam Khatoon—my two smudge-faced hiking buddies from the Dunda Mandal Hills—and waved and said goodbye to Fatima, who was sitting with tiny Halima cradled in her arms. I walked out of the tent with Yusuf by my side.

Everyone else in Yusuf's family was out doing things that needed doing, so I wasn't able to say real goodbyes to them. It felt odd that my intense and intimate experience with these people wouldn't be wrapped up with a neat and final moment of closure. I hoped no one would be upset that I vanished before having a chance to exchange last words and handshakes or hugs. It was only sixteen months later, when I would go back to visit these families again, that I realized what they seemed to know at the time: that goodbye didn't have to be a big deal, that closure was irrelevant, since our relationships were not coming to an end; I could leave the mountains, leave India, and not return for a year or two, and it would seem like we had only parted for a few hours.

I said goodbye to Yusuf one last time as we neared Dhumman and Jamila's tent and watched him stride off over the rolling grasses with the familiar bounce to his step and his *lathi* tucked under his arm.

I stood with Jamila and Appa outside their tent. Sharafat and Goku, who were working on the *chhappar* nearby, came back over once more to wait with us. I hoped Dhumman would return before I left but, knowing well how his plans were prone to changing at the last minute, there was really no guessing when he might be back. I couldn't wait for him.

In my halting Hindi, I told Jamila that her family was wonderful and that I would never forget them. She smiled and laughed, as though what I'd said was at once obvious and ridiculous, and told me to come back and see them soon. I hugged Sharafat and shook hands with the women, looking each in the eyes in a way that I hoped could convey my fondness for them better than I could in words. "You are our brother," Appa said with a sad smile. Dhumman didn't arrive.

I shouldered my pack and told my friends I would surely visit again, then turned and headed away from the camp. Despite one strange but deeply-held superstition I have, which is rooted in the Biblical story of Lot's wife and the Greek myth of Orpheus and Eurydice, when I reached a hill from where I knew I'd have a perfect vista of the huts and the tents and the family that had taken me in so completely, I couldn't help it. I looked back.

I moved quickly across the rolling alpine grasses, dropped over the pass, and zigzagged down the steep switchbacks that cut through the treeless bowl. I entered the tight canyon and passed the spot where the dead tree had fallen on the young buffaloes. After crossing the creek several times, I walked through our Dodi Tal camp, around the little lake, and beyond. Without pausing, I passed Manji, and continued descending along the main trekking route, just as we had done when we'd gone to fetch more supplies. But this time, as each step brought me closer to the river, closer to Sangam Chatti, closer to the road, I knew I wouldn't be hiking back up.

I pushed on, awash in memories of my friends, with the ache of their absence wedged in my chest and the pleasure of the trail beneath my feet.

EPILOGUE

🌱

T he following year, as the spring of 2010 approached, Uttarakhand's forest department once again declared that the Van Gujjars and their buffaloes would be banned from the meadows of Govind National Park. Dhumman, Jamila, and the rest of the family were thrust into a familiar and difficult dilemma. As much as they discussed the subject, they had no idea whether the park authorities would ultimately back down and allow their tribe into Govind, as they eventually did in 2009, or whether they would follow through on their threat.

Recalling the physical and emotional hardships of the migration of 2009, when I travelled with them, Dhumman, Jamila, Yusuf, and Roshni agreed on two things: that they would not return to Kanasar, and that before packing up and leaving the Shivaliks, they would decide where, exactly, they were going—whether to their traditional meadows or somewhere else.

As April neared, the forest department showed no signs of weakening its resolve. Feelings of insecurity gripped the Van Gujjars' jungle *deras*. My friends had little faith that the gates to Govind would swing open at the last minute, and they were not eager to endure the kind of tension they'd experienced on the road last time, waiting and praying for mercy from those in positions of power.

After much deliberation, my friends settled on a radically different approach than they had chosen in 2009. Dhumman and Yusuf made arrangements with a farmer near Kalsi—at the edge of the plains, where the Yamuna River emerges from the mountains—to stay near his fields from April through September, and to purchase fodder in bulk at reasonable rates. They wouldn't even try to go to the high meadows.

As it turned out, by the end of April, not long after the families reached Kalsi, Uttarakhand's chief minister, Ramesh Pokhriyal Nishank, made a surprising decision to intervene on behalf of the nomads, ordering the forest department to let them into Govind National Park. Unfortunately for my friends, they had already committed to the deal that they had made to stay at Kalsi and would have lost substantial amounts of money had they bailed out on it.

While camped for months near Kalsi, their fodder expenditures were offset by the ready access they had to markets where milk sold for decent prices. Financially, they more or less broke even. The heat, they said, had been unbearable, and they doubted whether all of their buffaloes would have survived had they not been able to spend hours immersed in the river each day. Otherwise, life at Kalsi was easy. In some ways, Appa told me, it had been too easy: since they hadn't travelled up and down to the Himalayas and hadn't spent the summer active at high altitudes, they and their animals were noticeably out of shape when they returned to the jungles of the Shivaliks. After a relatively sedentary few months, the buffaloes had a harder time moving through the hills, and Appa and her brothers and sisters found it more difficult than usual to climb trees and lop leaves. Even before that summer had ended, Dhumman and Jamila agreed that they would try to head back to their ancestral meadows at Gangar the following year, no matter what.

They successfully returned to their traditional summer meadows in 2011, and in subsequent years with no real problems. While the forest department has not stopped the Van Gujjars from reaching Govind National Park, neither has it granted them official permission to enter it. The government insisted it was acting only out of humanitarian concern, not because it was compelled by the Forest Rights Act, or any other law, to let the nomads in. In fact, Dhumman said that when he, Yusuf, Alfa, and other permit-holders went to pay their summer grazing taxes, the authorities took their money but refused to issue them the paper permits and receipts that would prove they made their payments. It appeared to be an exercise in the same kind of logic that impelled Dhumman to pay his grazing taxes at Gangar when he was really at Kanasar, but in reverse: by withholding the receipts, as far as the written record was concerned, there were no nomads in the park—even though they spent the entire summer there.

Dhumman and Yusuf were sure that this was part of a forest department plan to show that Van Gujjars had abandoned their meadows, and were hence abdicating their ability to assert claims under the Forest Rights Act, which has not yet been fully implemented in Uttarakhand. Manto agreed with their suspicions, but reassured them that such a ploy would have no impact on how the Forest Rights Act was applied, since the only thing that mattered was whether a family could prove their ancestral use of the land dating from at least seventy-five years prior to December 2005; in other words, as far as the Forest Rights Act was concerned, it didn't matter one bit if it looked on paper like the meadows had been empty as of 2011.

Despite several seasons of minimal hassles on the migration, my friends aren't convinced that their problems are over, nor are they confident that their ability to access their summer pastures is truly secure. Though they feel like the immediate danger has retreated a bit, they take it year by year. They know that their fate is largely reliant on the whims of people and agencies that they've learned they can't always trust. The only thing that might be able to change that is the proper implementation of the Forest Rights Act—though there is no telling when that will happen, and no guarantee that the Van Gujjars will ultimately be covered by it, though they meet all of the criteria as laid out in the law.

My friends' lingering insecurities seem entirely justified. In April 2015, just before publication of this book in India, I asked Namith to speak with Uttarakhand's chief wildlife warden, D.S.

Khati, who I was having trouble reaching by phone from the United States. I wanted to get an update on the forest department's current position concerning the Van Gujjars' right to enter Govind National Park. Namith reported that Khati told him that, while no decision had been made to block the nomads in 2015, neither would the forest department officially issue their seasonal grazing permits. Khati added that he, personally, opposed their presence in the park. He reiterated the old argument that Van Gujjars who winter in UP have no rights to use forest lands in Uttarakhand, and he went even further, denying that Van Gujjars are a traditional migratory community, because old documents that bolster the claims of the tribe refer to "Gujjars" not "Van Gujjars."

In fact, Khati's attitude toward the Van Gujjars goes against current conservation trends. Over the past several years, the global conservation community has begun to embrace the possibility that nomadic herders can be important partners in environmental protection projects. Various United Nations agencies—including the UN Environment Program (UNEP), the UN Development Program (UNDP), and the Food and Agriculture Organization (FAO)—along with major international NGOs—such as the International Union for Conservation of Nature (IUCN)—now support a diverse array of collaborations between tribes and environmentalists.

As these organizations consider how to achieve international goals for both economic development and ecological sustainability, which are often opposing aims, they have concluded that "many traditional land management practices have proven to be more economically viable than more 'modern' alternatives, whilst simultaneously providing conservation benefits." Pastoralists in particular, they note, often create economic value—their livelihoods—in ways that are environmentally sustainable by maintaining "herding strategies that mimic nature." Put simply, if the idea is to encourage economic growth without harming the planet, it's looking more and more as though traditional and indigenous herding communities are already part of the solution. Additionally, with their intimate knowledge of their ancestral lands, they have been welcomed as key players in innovative efforts to protect endangered species that live in their territory, from snow leopards in the mountains of Afghanistan and Pakistan, to lions in the Kenyan savannah.

In other words, it's becoming clearer and clearer to the scientific establishment and to conservation groups, including many of those who have been accused in the past of promoting "green imperialism," that nomadic herders are not the indisputable threat to the environment that they were once assumed to be. While there may be certain situations in certain regions in which traditional herding methods are no longer sustainable, due to the impact of contextual factors such as climate change, industrialization, or overpopulation, much closer scrutiny must be applied on a case-by-case basis before writing off nomadic pastoralism as ecologically destructive. After all, these communities generally treat the environment as though their lives, and their futures, depend upon it, providing a lesson that those of us in the developed and developing world would be wise to pay attention to.

On a more personal note, I have been back to see my Van Gujjar family three times since I hiked out of the Himalayas at the end of May 2009.

On my first visit, in October 2010, Namith and I once again took the bus from Dehradun to Mohand, then found a ride in the back of a milk truck along the rutted road that is the informal boundary between the forests and the fields. Though I had only been here twice before, the journey felt surprisingly familiar, as though the details of the route had been permanently imprinted in my memory. We got out of the truck at the same spot in the middle of nowhere as we had on our previous visits, and began hiking toward the hills, up the wide, rocky *rao*. This time, there was water flowing in it, and there were several spots where we had to wade across a gently-flowing, calf-high stream. The sun was shining in a cloudless sky, and it was hot, though not as brutal as it had been when we'd come in April of the previous year.

I was excited but nervous, eager to see my friends, though uncertain as to what our reunion would be like. Would it feel as natural, as normal, to be with them again as it had during the migration? Or, now that we were no longer engaged in an all-consuming activity with a shared goal, would it feel different, more awkward for my long absence?

As we neared the high, steep bank atop which Yusuf's *dera* sat, we saw three small children watching us through the trees. Before I had a chance to guess who they were, one of them called my name, surprising me by how quickly they recognized me, and from such a distance that my features couldn't have been very distinct. But then, of course, not many people come hiking up this *rao* carrying a backpack.

Our reception couldn't have been more perfect: Yusuf and his family were thrilled to see us—and they were busy preparing to perform an improvised veterinary maneuver on a horse with an infected leg. So, after the hugs and handshakes and smiles, but before we could sit together and share chai, the horse had to be wrestled and held to the ground while a treatment involving herbs and a red-hot *patal* blade was administered.

We didn't linger long at Yusuf's, since we wanted to reach Dhumman and Jamila's *dera* before dark. They'd moved to a place about a mile away from the hut where I had first met them, up a different little tributary of the same main *rao*. They were still surrounded by jungle-covered hills, only their new hut was a bit larger than their old one.

Their welcome was as warm as I could have hoped for, and I instantly felt at home, as though only a week or two had passed since I had last seen these friends that I'd come to know so well. Sharafat and Appa were particularly thrilled at my return: Sharafat made sure to sit right beside me, occasionally placing his hand on my arm, as we all drank *chai* and exchanged news; Appa was desperate to talk about the despair she felt as her divorce remained unsettled and her future remained in a frustrating state of suspended animation. Dhumman greeted me with visible, if understated, joy. The fact that we hadn't had a chance to say goodbye before I left the meadows at Kanasar didn't matter at all; he'd been confident we would see each other again.

As we began catching up, there was one thing I wanted to know about above all else. The yearling. The one with the broken leg. Had it survived?

No, Dhumman said. Despite their best efforts, the leg had become infected, and there was nothing they could do about it. The young buffalo had been buried at Kanasar. Hearing this, I felt deflated; I had hoped to walk among the herd and see a fully-grown animal with a slightly crooked gait, happily munching on leaves.

I switched the subject, wondering whether they'd had trouble migrating to the mountains in the spring, and I was surprised to learn about how they had spent the summer near Kalsi instead of trying to reach their meadows.

Aside from that, and their new hut, not much of significance seemed to have changed since I'd last seen them a year-and-a-half earlier.

The next chance I had to visit them was almost exactly two years later, in October 2012, and by that time, several things leapt out at me as being different than they'd been before.

Unlike the pristine peacefulness that had characterized the Van Gujjars' forest world during my previous experiences in it, this time a palpable tension gripped the *deras* of all the nomads we met, and the Shivaliks seemed on the verge of conflict.

Farmers from villages just outside the forest had decided to claim sections of the jungle for themselves, eager to cut down and sell the wood from the trees whose leaves the Van Gujjars use to feed their buffaloes. A couple of weeks earlier, the villagers had set up barriers in the *raos*, trying to physically block the Van

Gujjars from returning from the Himalayas, then they threatened to burn their huts to the ground and attack their families with force, if that's what it took, to force the nomads to leave the lands on which they had a legal right to live.

By the time I got there, the Van Gujjars had settled back into their huts, but remained on alert; many more villagers than usual were tramping around the jungle, removing wood and asserting their presence in a manner that bore a tacit warning. For the first time, the Van Gujjars here feared being driven from their ancestral territory by someone other than the forest department. As the situation escalated, they appealed to the police and the forest rangers, who stepped in to avert an immediate eruption of violence, and instructed the villagers and the nomads to face off in court, not in physical combat. By the time I left the jungle, nothing had been resolved, but later, as the case was about to appear before a judge, the villagers backed down and the troubles were successfully diffused. Since then, with the implementation of the Forest Right Act in Uttar Pradesh—which is far ahead of its implementation in Uttarakhand—the Van Gujjars began to feel they had little to fear from their settled neighbors.

While not as dramatic as the threats from the villagers, some of the other changes that I saw in the jungle in the fall of 2012 were equally notable and most likely of greater significance for Van Gujjar culture in the long run. For instance, many more Van Gujjars were driving more motorbikes up the *raos* and along forest paths than ever before (though neither Dhumman, Yusuf, nor their children had acquired one), bringing the sounds of motors and machines into places where they previously didn't exist. And, back in 2009, Dhumman had owned his family's sole mobile phone; now, all of the older kids had them too, despite the lack of connectivity and the rare opportunity to charge them. Sharafat had even loaded some videos onto his, though his screen was less than two inches wide by one inch high. He knew that this was something of questionable moral probity, but since the few music videos and sitcoms he possessed were all performed by Muslim entertainers, he rationalized that it was okay to watch them—as long as his father wasn't around. This was an all-new intrusion by the modern world, and it struck me as a radical one, like an irreparable tear in the veil of the forest and a portent of things to come.

Sharafat had gotten married about a year before my 2012 visit, but his wife was away with her family of origin when I was there, so I didn't meet her; for his part, Sharafat didn't seem any more enthused or disappointed about being married than he had when he was engaged—it was neither wonderful nor terrible, just a fact of life. Meanwhile, one of his worst fears had come to pass: he had fallen out of a tree while lopping leaves. Luckily, only his wrist had been broken, and it had healed well; by the time I saw him, he was again climbing into high branches to cut fodder for the herd.

Appa's divorce still had not been settled, and she was losing hope that it ever would be. Just when it seemed like the details were nearly worked out, her husband's family would change its demands. Appa had tried going back to her husband a couple of times, but was even more miserable with him than in a state of marital limbo, so she returned to her own family and steeled herself to wait for a resolution, however long it took.

The smaller kids, of course, had grown: little Salma was doing chores like sweeping and washing dishes; Yasin was chasing buffaloes and practicing smacking them with a *lathi*; Bashi had graduated from tending calves to milking and climbing trees; and Goku had become a competent cook and had transformed from a cautious leaf-cutter into a human thresher.

Since they were almost always out of mobile phone range, I had no direct contact with anyone in the family unless I was with them in person. Between visits, it was rare for me to hear any news about them. So I was surprised in the fall of 2013 when I got an email from Namith, saying that Appa had called him. His note was a bit vague, but it sounded like the family was dealing with an unexpected tragedy—from what Namith understood, Sharafat had cancer and was very sick. I wrote a number of messages to Namith, and to Manto, trying to get some clarity about Sharafat's condition, but the channels of communication were so murky that it was difficult to glean an accurate understanding of what was really happening until it was unequivocal. In early 2014, Sharafat—my younger/ older brother in the forest—died.

When I went back to visit the family in September 2014, I caught up with them while they were migrating down from the Himalayas. I wasn't sure how I would broach what I imagined would be a very sensitive subject, but I needn't have worried about it. Within two minutes of my arrival at their temporary camp on the side of the road, Dhumman asked me directly if I had heard about Sharafat. I said I had, and Dhumman and Jamila together told me how horrible it had been to see him struggle and suffer and pass away.

While his absence was obviously felt, the family had plenty of things to take their minds off their loss. For one, Jamila had had another baby about a year before Sharafat's death—an adorable little girl who was already toddling around on her own two feet. Goku had married and was visibly pregnant. Sharafat's widow, whose name was Mariam, had remarried his brother, Mir Hamza, providing a strong, smart, and cheerful match for the family's eldest son, who had been without his first wife for several years (if you recall, she was the sister of Appa's husband, and had returned to her family of origin when Appa left her husband).

Appa, who I had been looking forward to reconnecting with, was missing from the caravan; earlier in the year, her divorce had at last been finalized, and she had married again, this time to a good man who lived in the forest, not in Gandikhatta. She was with him and his family and their herd, moving down from their mountain meadow. I was able to speak with her for a couple of minutes on the phone, and when we hung up, I mentioned to Goku and Jamila that Appa sounded happy. "Yes, she is," Jamila said. "Very."

SELECTED REFERENCES

Baswan, B.S., Official letter written by B.S. Baswan, Secretary, Ministry of Tribal Affairs, Government of India, titled "Removal of Encroachments on Forest Land." Dated 18 October 2002.

Bhargav, Praveen and G.S. Rawat, "Site Inspection Report of Govind Sanctuary and National Park, Uttarakhand State." 26 August 2009, http://www .wildlifefirst.info/pdfs/pa_ifa/2_Final_Report_ Govind_NP.pdf

Borgerhoff Mulder, Monique and Peter Coppolillo, *Conservation: Linking Ecology, Economics, and Culture*. Princeton, NJ: Princeton University Press, 2005.

Brockington, Daniel and James Igoe, "Eviction for Conservation: A Global Overview." *Conservation and Society* 4(3), September 2006.

Davies, Jonathan, et al, *Conserving Dryland Biodiversity*. Nairobi: International Union for the Conservation of Nature, 2012.

Gadgil, Madhav and Ramachandra Guha, *Ecology and Equity: The Use and Abuse of Nature in Contemporary India*. London/New York: Routledge, 1995.

Gooch, Pernille, "A Community Management Plan: The Van Gujjars and the Rajaji National Park," in *State, Society and the Environment in South Asia*, S.T. Madsen. Psychology Press, 1999.

Gooch, Pernille, *At the Tail of the Buffalo: Van Gujjar Pastoralists Between the Forest and the World Arena*. Lund, Sweden: Lund University, 1998.

Gooch, Pernille, "Van Gujjar: The Persistent Forest Pastoralists." *Nomadic Peoples*, 8 (2), 2004.

Gooch, Pernille, "Victims of conservation or rights as forest dwellers: Van Gujjar pastoralists between contesting codes of law." *Conservation & Society*, vol. 7, issue 4, 2009.

SELECTED REFERENCES

Joshi, Ritesh and Rambir Singh, "Gujjar Community Rehabilitation from Rajaji National Park: Moving Towards an Integrated Approach for Asian Elephant (*Elephas maximus*) Conservation." *Journal of Human Ecology*, 28(3): 199-206 (2009).

Ministry of Environment & Forests, Government of India, Order titled "Traditional rights of tribals on forest lands—discontinuance of eviction of tribals thereof." Dated 21 December 2004.

National Human Rights Commission (India), Testimony related to Case Number 14971/24/97-98, recorded 19 February 1998.

National Human Rights Commission (India), Order related to Case Number 14971/24/97-98, Issued 4 March 1999.

National Human Rights Commission (India), Report related to Case Number 14971/24/97-98, Issued 12 December 2000.

Nusrat, Rubina, "Marginalization of Himalayan Pastoralists and Exclusion from their Traditional Habitat: A Case Study of Van Gujjars in India." *International Journal of Human Development and Sustainability*, 4(1) Spring, 2011.

Pallavi, Aparna, "Uttarakhand Gujjars Being Ousted Without Compensation." Indiatogether.org, 5 September 2008, http:// www.indiatogether.org/2008/sep/ hrt-gujjars.htm

Rao, A., and Michael J. Casimir, "Mobile Pastoralists of Jammu & Kashmir: A Preliminary Report." *Nomadic Peoples*, Number 10, April 1982.

Sharma, Anju, "Keep on the Grass." *Down to Earth*, 15 September 2001.

Sharma, Jyotsana, et al, "Forest utilization patterns and socio-economic status of the Van Gujjar tribe in sub-Himalayan tracts of Uttarakhand, India." *Forestry Studies in China*, 14 (1), 2012.

Singh, David Emmanuel, "Muslim Van Gujjars of Rajaji National Park in Uttaranchal, India," *Oxford Center for Mission Studies*, 2003.

Spence, Mark David, *Dispossessing the Wilderness: Indian Removal and the Making of the National Parks*. New York/Oxford: Oxford University Press, 1999.

Supreme Court of India, Order disposing of Writ petition number 78/79 Mohd. Shafi vs. State of U.P, dated 12 July 1990.

Thapliyal, Jotirmay, "Central panel takes note of curbs on Van Gujjars." *The Tribune*, Dehradun Plus Online Edition, 14 June 2010.

"Valley of Weeds." *Down to Earth*, http://www.downtoearth.org.in/ node/17792

West, Paige and Dan Brockington, "An Anthropological Perspective on Some Unexpected Consequences of Protected Areas," *Conservation Biology*, 20 (3), June 2006.

West, Paige, James Igoe, and Dan Brockington, "Parks and Peoples: The Social Impact of Protected Areas." *Annual Review of Anthropology*, Vol 35, 2006, www.forestrightsact.com

Zahler, Peter and George Schaller, "Saving More Than Just Snow Leopards." *The New York Times*, 1 February 2014.

ACKNOWLEDGMENTS

I owe a huge debt of gratitude to several people behind the scenes who helped make the research and writing of this book possible.

First, I'd like to thank Praveen Kaushal, known to many as Manto, who is the founder and executive director of the Society for the Promotion of Himalayan Indigenous Activities (SOPHIA). Without the generous support that he offered in countless ways, I never would have met Dhumman, Jamila and their family, and never would have been able to see this project through to the end. Our many conversations clued me in about numerous aspects of Van Gujjar life, as well as the larger socio-political situation in which they are immersed, all of which would have been much, much more difficult for me to uncover and understand on my own.

I'd also like to thank Dr. Pernille Gooch, whose field research among the Van Gujjars was an invaluable source of information about Van Gujjar culture, providing me with a rich and detailed glimpse into their world before I ever stepped foot into it. Much of the background information I present about Van Gujjars in this book is in some way rooted in or connected to her work. Moreover, the record that her papers provide has helped me track the ways in which Van Gujjar culture and their circumstances have changed over time, and helped me formulate relevant questions to ask about their lives today.

Though I will honor his wish to remain anonymous, I must thank my translator, "Namith," whose assistance during the migration was absolutely essential to my understanding of what was going on most of the time! I have great respect for the physical efforts he made and the discomforts he endured in the course of helping me cover this story.

Big thanks also go to the staff of SOPHIA, including Munesh, Nazim, Reena, and Joshi, who assisted me in various ways during my time in India. Also, thanks to Avdash Kaushal, head of Rural Litigation and Entitlement Kendra (RLEK), for several conversations as well as the copies of court documents that he provided to me, related to the Van Gujjars' expulsion from Rajaji National Park. I'd also like to thank Ben Lenzner, a photographer who once interned with RLEK and spent considerable amounts of time with the Van Gujjars, who offered me valuable advice before I undertook this project.

Of course, the greatest thanks of all go to the Van Gujjar families who welcomed me into their world: Dhumman, Jamila, Yusuf, Roshni, Alfa, Sakina, and all of their children, daughters-in-law, and grandchildren. They had to live with me, 24 hours a day, 7 days a week, from the lowland jungles to the Himalayan meadows, in the process giving me one of the most rewarding and unforgettable experiences I will ever have. None of this would have been possible without them. They will remain friends for life.

I'm also grateful to my own little family, Kelly and Luke, who encouraged me to undertake this adventure and attempt to make something meaningful from it. And I could not have done that without help from my ever-enthusiastic and resourceful agents, Allison Devereux, in New York, and Sherna Khambatta, in Mumbai, as well as my editor, Jessica Case, who has put her energies into making this a beautiful book—thank you all!